Management Consulting
in Africa

Kumarian Press Library of Management for Development

Managing Organizations in Developing Countries: A Strategic and Operational Perspective
by Moses N. Kiggundu

Reforming Public Administration for Development: Experiences from Eastern Africa
by Gelase Mutahaba

Public Service Accountability: A Comparative Perspective
edited by Joseph G. Jabbra and O. P. Dwivedi

Enhancing Policy Management Capacity in Africa
edited by Gelase Mutahaba and M. Jide Balogun

Vitalizing African Public Administration for Recovery and Development
by Gelase Mutahaba, Rweikiza Baguma, and Mohamed Halfani

Public Administration in Small and Island States
edited by Randall Baker

Managing Quality of Care in Population Programs
edited by Anrudh K. Jain

Improving Family Planning Evaluation: A Step-by-Step Guide for Managers
by José García-Núñez

Management Dimensions of Development: Perspectives and Strategies
by Milton J. Esman

Breaking the Cycle of Poverty: The BRAC Strategy
by Catherine H. Lovell

Getting to the 21st Century: Voluntary Action and the Global Agenda
by David C. Korten

Democratizing Development: The Role of Volutary Organizations
by John Clark

Keepers of the Forest: Land Management Alternatives in Southeast Asia
edited by Mark Poffenberger

The Water Sellers: A Cooperative Venture by the Rural Poor
by Geoffrey D. Wood and Richard Palmer-Jones with M. A. S. Mandal, Q. F. Ahmed, and S. C. Dutta

Opening the Marketplace to Small Enterprise: Where Magic Ends and Development Begins
Ton de Wilde and Stijntje Schreurs with Arleen Richman

A Dragon's Progress: Development Administration in Korea
edited by Gerald E. Caiden and Bun Woong Kim

Management Consulting in Africa

Utilizing Local Expertise

editor
Frederick J. Kaijage

Kumarian Press

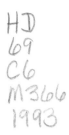
Management Consulting in Africa: Utilizing Local Expertise

Published 1993 in the United States of America by Kumarian Press, Inc.,
630 Oakwood Avenue, Suite 119, West Hartford, Connecticut 06110-1529 USA.

Cover design by Beth Gorman

Production supervised by Jenna Dixon, Bookbuilder

Text design by Jenna Dixon
Copyedit by Linda Lotz
Typeset by Rosanne Pignone
Proofread by Jolene Robinson
Index by Paul Kish

Printed in the United States of America on recycled acid-free paper by
Thomson-Shore. Text printed with soy-based ink.

Library of Congress Cataloging-in-Publication Data

Management consulting in Africa : Utilizing local expertise / editor, Frederick J.
    Kaijage.
          p.   cm. — (Kumarian Press library of management for
    development)
    Includes bibliographic references and index.
    ISBN 1-56549-017-7 (alk. paper). — ISBN 1-56549-016-9 (pbk. : alk.paper)
    1. Business consultants—Africa.   I. Kaijage, Fred J.   II. Series.
    HD69.C6M366   1993
    001'.096—dc20   92-34559

---

97   96   95   94   93   5   4   3   2   1
First printing, 1993

Contents

Preface

This book is part of the contribution of the African Association for Public Administration and Management (AAPAM) to the development of the management consulting profession on the African continent. The papers selected and edited for this volume were originally presented at two AAPAM workshops for senior-level policymakers on the optimal utilization of management consultants in Africa. The first of the workshops took place in Arusha, Tanzania, in August 1987, and the second was held a year later in Accra, Ghana. In publishing this book, we are fulfilling the wish of the participants in the Accra workshop, who strongly recommended that such a task be undertaken.

The two AAPAM workshops brought together senior-level policymakers and a number of well-known African consultants. The latter, all of whom are seasoned management consultants, acted for the most part as resource persons. The workshops helped to sensitize and provide useful knowledge and skills to senior administrators and managers on the optimal use of consultants. They also helped to launch the consultants on a path toward the establishment of networks among themselves. Indeed, within a year after the Accra workshop, AAPAM sponsored an impact assessment mission to nine African countries. The objectives were to help enhance the performance of different consulting groups, facilitate the development of African consultants' networks, develop a roster of African consultants, develop a manual of tips on management consultancy in Africa, and initiate the formation of national associations of management consultants.

Subsequent to the work of that mission, two important events have taken place. The first was an AAPAM-sponsored training needs study, which identified training needs in eight areas of management consultancy. The second was the launching of a continentwide association of African management consultants in July 1990 at an AAPAM-sponsored meeting of African management consultants in Kampala, Uganda. The formation of national associations of management consultants is also forging ahead.

One hopes that, in the long term, the above-mentioned initiatives on the part of AAPAM and its members, including the publication of this book, will remove the impediments to the optimal utilization of management consultants in Africa that arise, for the most part, out of misperceptions and lack of adequate knowledge about the consulting profession on the part of senior administrators and managers. I also believe that practitioners as well as students of management consultancy in Africa will find the book an invaluable source of knowledge and inspiration.

This book is very much a product of joint efforts, involving not only the authors and myself as editor, but other individuals and agencies as well. I express my sincere appreciation to all those who made it possible for this work to see the light of day in its present form. First of all, I thank the Canadian International Development Agency (CIDA) and the Commonwealth Fund for Technical Cooperation (CFTC), whose generous grants made it possible for AAPAM to sponsor the Arusha and Accra workshops and fund the publication of this book. I am also grateful to Rwekaza Mukandala, Mohamed Halfani, Gelase Mutahaba, and Lettice Rutashobya for their helpful comments. However, they bear no responsibility for whatever shortcomings the reader might detect in this work. I owe a vast debt to Daines-Mary Kuhanga, who made a valiant effort, sometimes at the cost of her sleep, to ensure that the manuscript was impeccably typed and in good time. Finally, special thanks go to Professor Lou Hamman and his colleagues in the Global Studies program at Gettysburg College, who provided both the facilities and the collegial environment that made it possible for me to put the finishing touches on this work.

Frederick J. Kaijage

About the Contributors

Ason Bur. Until recently was Deputy Governor, Benin State, Nigeria. Formerly Director-General, Management Services and Training Division, Federal Civil Service Commission, Nigeria.

Mike B. Durodola. Director of Consultancy and Extension Services, Administrative Staff College of Nigeria (ASCON).

S. M. B. Fye. Director-General, Management Development Institute, Kanifing, the Gambia.

G. A. Haldane-Lutterodt. Senior Lecturer, Ghana Institute of Management and Public Administration (GIMPA); formerly Executive Secretary, Management Services, Office of the Head of Civil Service, Ghana.

Ijuka Kabumba. Managing Director, National Insurance Corporation, Uganda; formerly Principal Lecturer, Uganda Institute of Public Administration.

Frederick J. Kaijage (editor). Associate Professor of History, University of Dar es Salaam, Tanzania, specializing in labor studies.

Joseph E. Kariuki. Until his death in 1991, Mr. Kariuki was a private management consultant based in Lusaka, Zambia; previously Director of CAFRAD and the Kenya Institute of Public Administration.

Talala Mbise. Senior Consultant, Eastern and Southern African Management Institute (ESAMI), Arusha, Tanzania.

Samuel K. Mtali. Office of the President, United Republic of Tanzania.

G. C. M. Mutiso. Managing Director, Mutiso Consultants Limited, Nairobi, Kenya; formerly, Associate Professor, Department of Government, University of Nairobi, Kenya.

Ngure Mwaniki. Managing Director, Mwaniki Associates Limited, a management consultancy firm based in Nairobi, Kenya.

James Nti. Chief Technical Adviser, Management Development Institute, the Gambia; formerly Director, Ghana Institute of Management and Public Administration (GIMPA).

Owino Nisa Ochieng. Private Consultant based in Addis Ababa, Ethiopia; previously held senior positions with the United Nations and the African Development Bank.

William H. Shellukindo. Principal Secretary, Office of the Prime Minister and First Vice President, United Republic of Tanzania.

P. S. P. Shirima. Managing Consultant, Training and Development Consultants, Arusha, Tanzania; previously Principal Consultant, Eastern and Southern African Management Institute (ESAMI), Arusha, Tanzania.

Hilda Kokuhirwa Sinkonde. Private consultant and adjunct professor, Yale University, Connecticut, USA.

Donald C. Sock. Lecturer in Management, Management Development Institute, Kanifing, the Gambia.

Owodunni Teriba. Chief of Socio-Economic Research Division, United Nations Economic Commission for Africa (ECA), Addis Ababa, Ethiopia; formerly Professor of Economics, University of Ibadan, Nigeria.

Introduction

FREDERICK J. KAIJAGE

This collection of essays on management consulting in Africa constitutes a culmination of persistent efforts on the part of many African governments, organizations, and individuals to harness and foster the growth of African expertise. Our belief is that this important indigenous resource has a significant, if not decisive, role to play in Africa's quest for economic and social development.

As early as 1974, the Organization of African Unity (OAU), the United Nations Economic Commission for Africa (ECA), the African Development Bank (AfDB), and the African Training and Research Center in Administration for Development (CAFRAD) organized a joint meeting on the utilization of African experts and resources of technical experience. One of the main themes of that meeting was the training and effective utilization of African consultants. Taking stock of available consultancy resources was regarded by the meeting participants as an important first step in this direction. Follow-up action by the organizers of that historic meeting has also been taken. In 1975, for example, CAFRAD organized its first workshop for its consultants, where the idea of creating a roster of African experts was adopted. In 1978 the ECA commissioned a survey of existing consultancy firms, organizations, and individuals in the eastern and southern African subregion. That survey, directed by Ngure Mwaniki, a contributor to this book, was the result of

1

a decision made in a joint ministerial meeting held in Lusaka, Zambia, the year before. The meeting participants had agreed to promote, within the framework of collective self-reliance, the enhancement of the sub-region's consultancy capability, which would assist the cooperating states in their development endeavors.[1] Also, a quest for greater national and regional self-sufficiency in matters pertaining to African development, including professional expertise, constituted a major thrust of the 1980 Lagos Plan of Action. The consuming desire behind all these initiatives was to steer Africa away from dependence on foreign expertise in its development endeavors.

Subsequent to the ECA survey, efforts have been made to organize African consultants across national boundaries in order to lend them greater visibility, mobilize their cooperative efforts, foster a cross-fertilization of ideas among them, and involve them in a collective search for solutions to the problems of their profession. At the same time, the training of African consultants in different disciplines has been moving apace both within formal institutions and on the job. Despite these commendable efforts, however, the consulting profession in Africa, especially in the field of management, is still a far cry from the vibrant and effective agent of change that it is intended to be.

The African Association for Public Administration and Management (AAPAM) has been charged, among other things, with the responsibility of promoting the development of capacity and capability in public administration and management in Africa. AAPAM is fully cognizant of the role that management consulting can play in the fulfillment of this objective. Following up on the deliberations of an expert group meeting it organized in 1986 at Badagry, Nigeria, AAPAM chose the improvement of the technical competence of African management consultants as a major area of concentration. Its role was expected to be a catalytic one, played through active collaboration with governments and other public and private agencies interested in the management consulting profession. As a starting point, AAPAM focused on enhancing the utilization of the resources that were already available. Thus the theme of the two AAPAM workshops on which this book is based was optimal utilization of indigenous management consultants in Africa.

In selecting that theme, AAPAM was aware of the problems complicating the use of existing management consultancy resources in Africa. One of the most persistent problems is the widespread negative attitude on the part of governments, public administrators, and managers toward the use of consultancy services, local as well as foreign. Second, there is a pervasive sense of ambivalence toward using indigenous consultants; non-African consultants are generally preferred. Third, even when consultancy services are employed, the consultants' recommendations are not always implemented. And fourth, the capability and competence of some individuals who pass for management consultants leave much to be desired, a factor that tends to aggravate the first three problems. It is these issues that AAPAM has had its eye on while trying to implement its action program on optimal use of management consultants in Africa.[2]

Management consultancy is a helping profession that intervenes to lend greater efficiency and vitality to an organization. It accomplishes this by either investigating and analyzing the organization's problems and prescribing solutions or infusing new ideas, including helping an apparently problem-free organization to renovate its structures or revitalize its processes by adopting new up-to-date management techniques. Management consultancy is therefore a catalytic agent for purposeful change. In Africa, where there is an incessant yearning for rapid economic and social transformation, management consultancy has a significant role in the continent's development endeavors. Although management consultancy is a science with universally applicable principles, some of the profession's manifestations are determined by the cultural milieu within which it operates. Culture in this context is broadly applied to include environmental, economic, political, and social processes.   •

In order to put the present collection of essays in their proper perspective, a brief review of the nature of the African management environment is needed. This review is handled at two levels: the salient issues pertaining to African development in the postindependence period, and the general tendencies in African organizations. In other words, the focus is on both the macro- and micro-level issues relating to management in Africa. Particular attention is paid to the public sector because of its conspicuous role in Africa's development endeavors.

The following discussion is not meant to be exhaustive; it is intended to isolate critical issues that, in my estimation, constitute major determinants of management processes in Africa. Given the complexity and diversity of the African socioeconomic landscape, I am well aware of the risks involved in embarking on an exercise in global analysis. But because of the common historical experience shared by the African countries, I believe that the risk is worth taking.

The Postindependence Environment

During the first decade of African independence, in the 1960s and early 1970s, the continent was optimistic about its prospects for economic and social development. This optimism was probably not unjustified, given Africa's resource potential and what was, in retrospect, a relatively favorable international economic and political climate. Africa enjoyed an atmosphere of general goodwill on the part of the rest of the world community, including the rich and powerful. African states, acting on behalf of their citizenries, demonstrated unshaken confidence in their ability to direct the course of their countries' development. They consequently created a plethora of institutions that would serve as vehicles for the development process. They complemented these with various forms of interventionist policy instruments. Ambitious programs and projects, under the direction of the new institutions, were undertaken. Substantial foreign grants and loans were sunk into a number of these programs and projects to supplement the resources that could be mobilized from within. The result of these developments has been the creation of a large public sector in the different African countries, irrespective of their professed ideological persuasions or the political rhetoric in vogue.[3]

Africa's rather unrestrained institution building naturally created a demand for managerial resources beyond what was readily available locally. In most countries this meant, in the initial period, either dependence on foreign management or recruitment of ill-prepared and inexperienced local managers, most of whom had to operate by rule of thumb. The young institutions had few if any management traditions to draw on and, as often as not, considerations other than economic rationality prevailed in the running of some institutions. The public enterprises were progressively turned into instruments for the exercise of political patronage; many senior appointments were based on political loyalty and support rather than managerial capability. This phenomenon can be characterized as the crisis of African management in its infancy. The adverse effects of this crisis are what management consultancy in Africa has had to contend with. But largely because of the realities relating to the availability and utilization of local expertise, and also because of donor pressure, most consultancy services have been provided by foreign firms and individuals.

The Present Environment

As we move into the 1990s, management in African institutions faces a serious crisis in its adolescence that threatens to dwarf the crisis of its infancy. The background of this crisis starts with a well-known, almost hackneyed, story. It arguably emanates from the oil shocks of the 1970s, which set in motion successive world economic recessions that have hit Africa very hard. The African side of the story is now a familiar one and has been the subject of penetrating analyses: The diminution of foreign earnings, the debt crisis, a perilously impaired capacity to import, and inflationary pressures in the domestic economies have all exerted tremendous pressure on the domestic social order.[4] In terms of the African management experience, the crisis has brought in its wake two major challenges: the need to reexamine the current institutional arrangements, and the pressure of having to manage with diminishing resources.

The beleaguered African states have approached, cap in hand, both multilateral and bilateral donor agencies for assistance to get out of the crisis. But the miserly aid agencies, led by the World Bank and the International Monetary Fund (IMF), insist on watching their pennies and will not part with their money without imposing conditions that some analysts consider to be ideologically determined and of questionable efficacy. Again, the story is a familiar one. Conditionality and structural adjustment are familiar, if controversial, household words in present-day Africa. No less than thirty African countries have had to accept donor-driven policy reforms in return for loans and grants.[5]

For African management, the most pertinent category of donor conditionality has been the redefinition of the state's role in economic management. The prevailing orthodoxy among Western industrialized countries, which inspires donor policy, is that market forces are a more efficient allocator of resources than the state. Those who perceive the African state as the principal agent of economic and social transformation are now on the defensive. African countries that want to take advantage of international financing must agree to free up market mechanisms by curtailing the role of the state in the economy, thus stepping up the role of the private sector. Privatization is another concept that is currently in vogue. So although established institutions die hard, African institutional arrangements are in for a radical restructuring, and there are already signs of the reallocation of roles in African economies.[6]

These externally imposed policy reforms, especially the assault on the public sector, mean that many African countries must undertake a fundamental review of their current institutional arrangements as well as major reforms, if not transformations, of their managerial structures and processes. With or without the IMF and the World Bank, many African countries, because of the economic crisis, now regard some of their public-sector organizations as albatrosses hanging around their necks. Some have been, or are in the process of being, eliminated; others are being restructured to varying degrees. In the process, new opportunities are emerging for the private sector.

The nascent reconstitution of the African organizational order is creating challenges as well as opportunities for African management consulting. The profession is expected, or should be called upon, to contribute to the formulation of new institutional arrangements and to assist governments as well as public-sector managers in coping with the repercussions of the scaling down of organizations. This is an opportunity for African management consultants to be creative. In addition, the expansion of the private sector offers the possibility of new avenues for consultancy practice, especially on the part of public-sector consultants. Private-sector consultancy may be on the threshold of a process of regeneration, especially if governments are willing to consider it an industry and offer it incentives conducive to consultants' "mental investment"—in training and skills—in their enterprises.

Another dimension of the African crisis is that the tasks of African managers are daunting, in terms of both the magnitude of the problems they have to cope with and the nature of the challenges they have to rise to. The diminution of resources under budgetary pressures, at both macro and micro levels, means that a number of institutions, especially those that are service oriented, are preoccupied with survival at the expense of systematic, planned development. Resources for running programs and projects have all but dried up in many cases, forcing some organizations to institute retrenchment. "Cutback management" is probably the most appropriate expression for this phenomenon. In some instances, management by crisis threatens to be the order of the day.

It would be unfortunate if the crisis described in the foregoing pages were allowed to engender a sense of despondency or an acceptance of economic and social atrophy as Africa's preordained fate. Even under the stress that African economies are now experiencing, it behooves African governments, administrators, and managers to think of strategies for improving economic performance by restoring production in industry and agriculture, rehabilitating the decayed infrastructure, and improving Africa's export earnings, thereby alleviating the balance-of-payments crisis and ultimately improving the quality of life of the African population in general. Action is demanded not only in devising and implementing appropriate macroeconomic policies but also in reviewing organizational performance. This is the major challenge that African managers face. It would be unrealistic, however, to expect functionaries who are bogged down with the immense day-to-day problems of their organizations to rise to the demands of this challenge. Their challenge is therefore also the challenge of the African management consulting profession. There is a critical need for new ideas, creative solutions, and fresh approaches and techniques, all of which consultants worth their salt—as practitioners on the cutting edge of the management profession—should be able to deliver.

Organizational Effectiveness

The next set of issues pertains to the level of organizational function. It has been observed that in developing countries there is a considerable lack of organizational and management capabilities, and that the lack of effective organizations is a serious bottleneck to development.[7] This is as true for Africa as it is for the rest of the developing world. But it is one thing to accept this view and quite another to suggest that the typical African organization is so peculiar as to defy all norms of a modern organization. An unduly pessimistic view of African organizations has frequently been expressed. Hyden, for example, suggests that African organizations manifest low levels of predictability mainly because they do not operate on the basis of "scientific and instrumental rationality." Too many extraorganizational factors, especially the "economy of affection," often come into play. He goes on to provide a catalogue of the peculiar features of African organizations, including hiring and firing procedures, materials management, planning, decisionmaking, the communication process, and managerial attitudes toward technical matters. On all these counts, African organizations come off badly: Hiring and firing norms are seldom enforced; there is confusion between personal resources and organizational or public resources; the attitude toward plans is too flexible; decisionmaking is a weakly institutionalized function; there is only downward communication; and top managers tend to be ambivalent toward technical matters, delegating them to junior and inexperienced staff. Because of what he depicts as the peculiar character of African organizations, Hyden is opposed to "technique peddling" in Africa by Western management consultants.[8]

It would be difficult, if not futile, to contest the view that African organizations are an integral part of the history and culture of the continent, and that they are likely to manifest certain unique features in keeping with that history and culture. Hyden's misgivings about Western "technique peddling" and, implicitly, his call for creative problem solving on the part of African management consultants are therefore well-taken. In this context, his argument lends support to the advocacy statement that constitutes the underlying theme of the essays in this collection. However, the dichotomy between African and Western organizations is a somewhat false one. First, Hyden's view is, to some extent, impressionistic, insofar as it is not supported by incontrovertible evidence. Second, and more important, Africa's history is not exclusively African. Over centuries, especially since the late nineteenth century, the continent has been an integral part of Western expansionism, with all its economic, political, and cultural ramifications. There has been a large Western input into the molding of African organizations. But having said this, I must also add that although African and Western organizations may have common characteristics, the low levels of economic and social development as well as other historical and cultural forces have exerted their own influence on African organizations, as they have in the rest of the developing world. I disagree with Hyden only insofar as he overstates his case and discounts the impact of historically determined external influences.

Studies conducted in Africa and elsewhere in the Third World point to certain characteristics that have a negative impact on organizational effectiveness. Some of the characteristics that are relevant to Africa and that should therefore be the focal point for management consulting practice in the region have been summarized by Moses Kiggundu:[9]

- Centralized leadership and highly personalized management styles;

- Poor utilization of specialized personnel;

- Poor support services;

- Inefficient and costly operating levels, which exert financial pressure on an organization's capital; and

- Lack of an effective human resources management function.

The last point is so important that it deserves further discussion. In Africa, where shortage of capital is proverbial, labor is the continent's most precious resource. Human resources development and utilization therefore assume a critical role in the development endeavor. Yet this is an area that leaves much to be desired. A recent World Bank report observed that the lack of adequate skills and experience to staff the modern public and private sectors constitutes a major constraint on Africa's development.[10] In fact, as Moses Kiggundu has so ably shown, the problem is deeper than that. Even the trained and experienced labor that does exist is not used to its best advantage, to say the least.[11]

According to Kiggundu, Africa and other developing countries find human resources utilization challenging because it requires specialized skills to undertake a comprehensive analysis of the internal and external factors that impinge on an organization's human resources. Such skills are in short supply. Thus in a typical African organization, the human resources management function is characterized by routine activities that focus on short-term considerations as opposed to activities that expand the horizons of the workforce and keep the organization's long-term strategic interests in view. Under these circumstances, African countries cannot expect to get good value for their efforts and investments in the development of their human resources. What is more, the current economic crisis has damaged the motivation of management and staff in African organizations. It is common knowledge that in most African countries, highly trained workers, including those in management positions, are poorly remunerated, which is a major disincentive. This problem not only leads to poor performance but has contributed to the African brain drain, with deleterious effects on managerial capacity and capability in many organizations.[12]

There are problems with other management functions as well. In financial management, attempts to inculcate financial discipline are seriously undermined as much by persistent budgetary pressures as by endemic corruption in high places. Existing marketing techniques, adopted essentially from Western industrialized countries, are hardly suitable in a situation of chronic poverty on the part of the majority of the African population, whose consumer behavior is, at any rate, influenced by a different value system. The ever-widening gap in information technology leaves African organizations trailing their Western counterparts in terms of the effectiveness of their organizational and management information systems. And, in Africa's import-intensive manufacturing and transportation enterprises, the pervasive foreign exchange constraints render operations management systems extremely fragile.

The catalogue of problems in African organizations is apparently endless. But it would not be entirely fair to accuse those who run African organizations, whether they be politicians or technocrats, of a lack of seriousness. They have had to operate under exigencies brought upon them by paucity of resources, institutional arrangements in a state of flux, and a generally disabling environment. They cannot be absolved, however, from those mistakes that are not attributable to impersonal forces. As a bearer of specialized problem-solving skills, management consultancy in Africa ought to use its creativity to address the problems arising from the weaknesses in the different management functions of African organizations.

A final point regarding issues of interest to management consulting in Africa involves aspects of "development management." Of particular significance are community-based development activities in the rural areas. These are activities that, for the most part, take place outside the framework of formally constituted bureaucratic institutions, but, given the centrality of rural production in African economies, they are extremely important. Because some of the agencies concerned tend to make political capital out of such activities, these activities often entail a conflict of interests involving political parties, governments, aid agencies, nongovernmental organizations, and the local people themselves. Such conflict tends to divert the people's energies from the tasks that matter and consequently to hamstring development endeavors. The real challenge to African management consultants is to study the managerial imperatives of such activities and devise organizational forms, procedures, and processes that will harmonize the conflicting interests and mobilize rural developmental resources in such a way that real development takes place.

The Status of African Consulting

The foregoing discussion on African development issues and problems constitutes a compelling case for promoting a greater role for management consultancy in the African management and administrative processes. But, as the contributions to this book indicate, African management consulting itself is in need of revitalization in order to effectively handle the calls upon its resources.

Before examining the problems that bedevil management consulting in Africa, it is appropriate to start with the five characteristics that the AAPAM Arusha and Accra workshop participants identified as attributes of a good management consultant:[13]

1. A high level of knowledge and skills based on an appropriate academic discipline or set of disciplines;

2. Work experience, preferably in a managerial capacity;

3. Personal qualities befitting an individual who has to act in an advisory capacity, for example, tact and good communication skills;

4. A recognized and visible base, preferably a registered consulting firm or an institution of higher learning; and

5. Membership in a professional association that takes charge of accreditation, enforces a code of conduct, regulates fees, and generally maintains the integrity of the profession by separating the good and genuine from the quack and irresponsible.

The workshop participants also expressed the belief that, from the point of view of development strategy, Africa should develop adequate indigenous management consultancy capacity and capability instead of leaving the resolution of its organizations' problems to the tender mercies of international consultants. Indigenous consultants are better placed to understand the intricacies of the local situation, have a stake in the improved performance of African organizations, and are more readily available to help with the implementation of recommended measures. Moreover, their use usually does not involve expenditure of valuable foreign exchange.[14]

Only a few of those Africans who call themselves management consultants would pass the test according to the criteria set by the AAPAM workshops. And foreign consultants continue to dominate the practice on the continent. Where does the problem lie? The problem, as I see it, is twofold: (1) there are internal weaknesses in the management consultancy profession, and (2) African management consultants have to put up with a disabling environment—nationally and internationally.

Operating with scarce resources, most African management consultants lack the wherewithal necessary to build up the organizational structures that would allow them to conduct their practices at high standards of performance. The preponderance of capital-starved individual consultants—a good number of whom are unregistered—means that there is little integration of expertise to facilitate the multidisciplinary work that management consultancy assignments often demand. The weak capital base also implies deficiencies in such crucial working facilities as office space; supplies and equipment; computer and word-processing facilities; secretarial services; transport; and telex, facsimile, and telephone facilities.[15] It is no wonder, therefore, that save for a sprinkling of viable private firms, the most successful consultants in Africa are still found in public-sector consultancy organizations or in institutions of higher learning.

The second weakness internal to African management consultancy relates to inadequate skills and experience among many of those who pass for management consultants. This problem is, of course, related to the general shortage of specialized skills in Africa, an issue that has already been discussed. Resources and facilities for training are limited. What is more, even for those with the requisite training, exposure to complex and varying management situations is rather narrow. This limitation constrains consultants' ability to analyze and synthesize problems and their solutions, decide among alternative courses of action, and present their ideas and proposals in ways that encourage their clients to accept them. Some clients have even complained of having fallen victim to impostors masquerading as management consultants, who, in their quest for easy money, simply read through old documents and reproduced what others had already proposed.[16] Professional associations could play an important role in protecting both consultants and their clients from these frauds.

Much of what *could* be done nationally to advance the cause of the profession—in terms of policy initiatives and managerial and administrative practice—is not being done adequately. As a result, African management consultants operate in a generally disabling environment. Many managers tend to view consultancy as a luxury they cannot afford, especially under conditions of budgetary constraints. At best they seek consultancy services as an afterthought, usually at the behest of a foreign donor.[17] And when management consultancy services *are* employed, there is usually a tendency to ignore local talent, even where it is readily available, and use foreign consultants. In some countries, the situation is quite bad. A recent survey revealed, for example, that in Malawi, Zambia, and Zimbabwe (partly because of their proximity to South Africa), indigenous consultants stand no chance of success unless there is deliberate, positive government action to promote their services.[18] There are also deficiencies in resources and facilities for training (both formal and on the job) and in the availability of credit facilities, especially for young, struggling firms. As the last two chapters in this volume indicate, some governments are already implementing measures to promote indigenous management consultancy. Sadly, however, others either continue to give preference to foreign consultants or, like the proverbial ostrich, bury their heads in the sand while their indigenous consultants struggle single-handedly for survival against many odds.

The most serious constraint on the development of African indigenous consultancy capacity and capability is foreign competition. Preference for foreign consultants is not only a colonial legacy among African managers and administrators; for the most part, it is a result of donor pressure. Donors prefer consultants from their own countries either because they want to maintain control over the preparation of the projects they fund or because they wish to provide jobs for their nationals and consequently retain some of the aid money. It is also possible that die-hard racists within the donor community may have serious doubts about the consulting skills of African professionals. Even multilateral donor agencies, generally reputed for their cosmopolitan outlook, are not free from prejudice against African consultants. In general, the international donor community pursues policies and practices that are either openly discriminatory or transparently partial. They favor foreign consultants by means of unrealistically rigid selection criteria and demands that African consultancy organizations find difficult to meet. Sometimes there is a deliberately created information gap. It has been observed that, in some instances, consulting opportunities in Africa are publicized in the foreign media before African consultants get to know about them. They may then be forced to remain content with the subordinate role of subcontracting, even though they will have to do most of the work.[19]

Management consulting in Africa is a problem-ridden profession. The contributors to this volume offer suggestions on how to resolve these problems. Their prescriptions fall into two categories. The first has to do with positive policy measures that must be taken at the level of governments, including affirmative action, in support of indigenous management consultancy. Like any other infant industry, the indigenous management consulting profession deserves to be nurtured and protected. The second set of prescriptions entails collective action on the part of the consultants themselves in order to ensure protection and promotion of the collective interests of the profession.

The Contributions in This Book

This book is divided into four parts consisting of a total of fifteen chapters. The first part deals with contextual issues pertaining to management consulting in Africa. Some of the questions I raised in the foregoing pages are given a fuller treatment in this part. The second part consists of essays on important topics related to the organization and practice of management consulting in the African context. The third part consists of accounts of institutional experiences with management consultancy. Both national and international institutions are represented. The final part provides instructive information on management consulting in two African countries, one East African and one West African.

In Chapter 1, Kariuki calls for an enhanced role for African management consultants and therefore a deemphasis on the use of expatriate consultants, whose mission is often the promotion of foreign interests. African management consulting capabilities can be increased by overcoming managerial prejudice, lending the profession both administrative and material support, and, above all, training. Regarding the management consulting process, the author recommends constant interaction between the consultant and the client throughout all the stages of the assignment, especially in situations that demand basic changes. If the two parties work together, the client—who will have to implement and live with the changes—will find it easier to identify with the changes in question because he will have contributed to their initiation.

In Chapter 2, Mwaniki argues a compelling case for favoring indigenous as opposed to foreign management consultancy practice in Africa. He acknowledges weaknesses that constrain the development of indigenous management consulting in developing countries in general and African countries in particular. The major drawback in Africa is the failure on the part of consulting organizations to cooperate by sharing information and pulling their resources together in order to optimize their use. This perpetuates foreign domination of the profession. The author prescribes a set of remedial measures, the most important of which are: (1) training and appropriate utilization of those so trained, (2) policy support through legislative and other forms of governmental action, and (3) a spirit of collective self-help on the part of the indigenous management consultants themselves.

In Chapter 3, Mutiso provides an interesting historical account of consultancy, which originated from the need for specialized engineering information in the mining industry. Social science–based consulting, initially dominated by economists, emerged in the post–World War II period with the need for expertise in large-scale economic planning. It is this external economistic tradition of consulting that influenced and continues to influence the course of donor-aided projects in the Third World. Management consulting developed out of the external accountant tradition, when accounting firms discovered that they would earn more money by creating management consultancy units within their organizations. Citing the case of Kenya, Mutiso traces the development of management consulting since independence. The British-based multinational accounting firms have dominated in this process, although there is now an interesting scenario of rivalry between the multinational consultancy firms on the one hand and indigenous consulting organizations on the other.

The merits and demerits of employing the services of indigenous African as opposed to international or foreign management consultants are discussed by Kabumba in Chapter 4. Both options, says the author, carry possibilities of advantages as well as disadvantages for the client. On balance, however, Kabumba advocates an increased role for local consultants, mainly because they are cost-effective and, because of their deep knowledge of the local situation, they are more likely to recommend measures that will be in keeping with the realities of the client organization or country. The author prescribes measures that, in his estimation, would foster the development of indigenous consultancy resources.

In Chapter 5, Sinkonde addresses the gender dimension of management consulting in the African context. She examines factors that constrain women's participation in the profession. These factors are basically historical, relating to the place of women in human society in general and African society in particular. The few women in the formal employment sector occupy inferior, low-paying jobs. Very few have risen to managerial or executive positions. The few who have gained entry into management consultancy still face adverse social, cultural, and attitudinal factors that tend to encumber their career prospects. Family responsibilities, prejudice, stereotypical views of women's roles, and poor communication links among African women themselves are some of the serious constraints on the success of female consultants. All is not lost, however, says Sinkonde, for the situation can be remedied through education, training, and the creation of awareness.

Part II starts with a topical subject discussed by Haldane-Lutterodt in Chapter 6. Given the current moves toward greater privatization in Africa, the issue of organizing and operating a private consultancy facility is pertinent and timely. The author discusses the pros and cons of the different organizational forms for a private consultancy facility. The functional hierarchical type provides for specialization by management functions, but it is fraught with risks of conflict over functional priorities and is inappropriate for assignments of a multidisciplinary nature. The single-purpose or vertical organizational type would resolve the foregoing problems but, because it is project oriented, may upset the normal regular organization and impair the job security of the professional staff. A third type, the matrix organization, would maximize the strengths and minimize the weaknesses of the functional and single-purpose structures, which tend to be unidimensional in a multidimensional world. But even the matrix form is not problem free; it is susceptible to internal jurisdictional conflicts. Haldane-Lutterodt is inclined to recommend the contingency form, based on the particular factors operating in a given environment. The author essentially calls for creativity in designing an organizational form for a private consulting business. He also advises that attention be paid to external linkages, or what he terms "live channels," for a two-way flow of vital information.

In terms of operating a private consulting facility, Haldane-Lutterodt recommends that consultancy costs be determined and the mode of payment unambiguously agreed upon before an assignment begins. Also, the different elements of the management process—such as planning, organizing, and control—should be systematically handled. As much as possible, full advantage must be taken of such modern facilities as computers and word processors in order to cope with a complex and rapidly changing management environment in the African context.

In Chapter 7, Teriba poses a challenge to the African institutions of higher learning (IHLs). The consultancy potential of these institutions, he argues, has not been adequately exploited for reasons ranging from ignorance and prejudice on the part of potential clients to the ivory-tower mentality and academic purism on the part of some IHL inmates. Teriba contends that consultancy in IHLs can be conducted in an innovative manner so that it does not conflict with the main functions of teaching and research. It can provide opportunities for a cross-fertilization of ideas, for practical experience on the part of students and academic staff, and for generating funds for the institutions and their staff.

The author, drawing on his firsthand experience at the University of Ibadan, suggests ways of creating an enabling environment for consultancy practice in IHLs. He recommends the setting up of central consultancy units that, though organically linked to the parent institutions, operate on a commercial principle under the direction of full-time managers. A fair and equitable distribution of consultancy proceeds must be ensured.

The theme of collaboration between the consultant and the client, briefly addressed by Kariuki in Chapter 1, is developed further by Nti in Chapter 8, where he discusses the roles of consultants and clients in defining the terms of reference. Although, strictly speaking, the setting of terms of reference is the responsibility of the client, in the African context, where relatively few managers are appropriately trained, serious difficulties have arisen in this area. Terms of reference may prejudge or obscure major issues, or allow no room for flexibility on the part of the consultant. Both consultant and client have an interest in the terms of reference because a proper definition of the problem is the first step toward its resolution. Definition of the terms of reference is therefore a joint responsibility of the two parties. The author strongly recommends that African managers be trained in the skills of problem definition.

The same author lends consistency to his theme of collaboration and interaction between the consultant and client in Chapter 9, where he discusses the reporting and review process in management consulting. He suggests stages at which the dialogue between the two parties should be conducted, and under what circumstances the written as opposed to oral form of feedback is preferable. Dialogue is mutually beneficial. The consultant gets the opportunity to identify gaps, obtain additional information, test hypotheses, and make it easy for the client to accept the final recommendations. The client, on the other hand, can gain new perspectives regarding the problems of the organization.

Part III on institutional experiences opens with Chapter 10, in which Bur discusses the role of the Nigerian federal government's Management Services and Training Department, which is strategically located within the Federal Civil Service Commission. Since the commission enjoys an independent status, the department, as a supplier of management consultancy services to the entire public-service system, has the clout and credibility befitting a consultancy organization. There is an element of complementarity between the consulting and the training components of the department.

The Nigerian Management Services and Training Department has fostered a climate of mutual acceptance between private and public consultants by organizing forums for the exchange of views. It recruits competent staff and pursues a vigorous training and retraining policy to enhance the professional competence of its consultants in order to ensure that there is no "crisis of credibility" on the part of it clients. The department also aggressively defends its annual budget to avert any possible "crisis of effectiveness" in the delivery of its services.

Since, in the nature of things, the consultancy functions of a government consultancy organization are often routine, the author proposes an infusion of new ideas from the private sector that would enable public consultants to effectively handle consultancy services for the productive public sector of the economy. Public and private consultants must therefore work together for the common good.

In Chapter 11, Mbise and Shirima write on the consulting experience of the Eastern and Southern African Management Institute (ESAMI), a subregional center of excellence that provides training, consultancy, and research services to public and private organizations mainly in eastern and southern Africa. Reconstituted in 1980, ESAMI had originally been founded in 1974 to provide such services to organizations in the defunct East African Community. The membership of ESAMI is open to all states of the subregion, and it pulls together some of the best talent in the area. This is an excellent example of collective self-reliance in the provision of management consultancy services. Training, consultancy, and research at ESAMI are closely interlinked. Management consultancy has expanded by leaps and bounds lately, so ESAMI is in the process of establishing a full-fledged consultancy division. The authors show how, over time, the institute's consultants have moved away from the conventional "consultant engineering" model to the more effective "process consultancy."

The consulting experience at one of Africa's famous institutions, the Administrative Staff College of Nigeria (ASCON), is discussed by Durodola in Chapter 12. Among other things, the college provides senior-level training for executives in both the public and private sectors and undertakes research and consultancy. As in the case of ESAMI, the three functions are closely linked and mutually reinforcing. ASCON consults in specialized areas of management in the public sector and, in this regard, its work complements that of the Management Services and Training Department described by Bur in Chapter 10. In what I consider to be an instructive practice, the college also exports its consultancy services beyond Nigeria's boarders to help other African countries in need of its services.

Durodola recounts the trials and tribulations of consulting in an atmosphere of indifference, narrowness of perspective, and corruption on the part of many managements. Also, he expresses disappointment with the misallocation of the highly specialized management consultants trained by ASCON.

Drawing upon personal experience, Ochieng discusses in Chapter 13 the setting up and operating of an internal consultancy facility. He argues that internal consultancy facilites are more appropriate for problems that require a deep knowledge of highly complex internal relations and constraints within an organization. The facility can be effective, however, only if it is strategically placed and its role and status are unambiguously defined. The author provides the experience of the African Development Bank (AfDB), with occasional reference to developments in the United Nations. In both organizations, the purpose of setting up the internal consultancy units was to facilitate major structural and operational changes. The internal consultants worked hand in glove with the external consultants to work out and launch the changes. The internal consultants also played a crucial role, through dialogue and training, in overcoming the resistance to change on the part of both management and staff.

Two country experiences with management consultancy are provided in Part IV of the book. In Chapter 14, Shellukindo and Mtali survey the historical and the current situations regarding management consultancy in Tanzania. Starting in the mid-1970s, the Tanzanian government adopted an active policy of promoting the development of local management consultancy capacity and capability and utilizing it effectively. A rigorous clearance procedure was instituted to ensure that foreign consultants are engaged only when the appropriate expertise is not available locally.

The authors give vivid illustrations of how expensive and disastrous foreign consultancy can be. Administrative structures recommended by international consultants have had to be abandoned after painful experiences with their implementation; immense industrial capacity installed at the behest of foreign advisers has remained idle for decades; and voluminous consultancy reports, paid for with valuable foreign exchange, have gathered cobwebs on managers' shelves because they are not implementable. The authors are also critical of local "briefcase consultants," practitioners of no fixed abode whose credentials are dubious.

Shellukindo and Mtali argue that the utilization of management consultancy resources in Tanzania is less than optimal. Too many short-cut measures, such as appointment of task forces and commissions of inquiry, are being used to deal with organizational problems. This smacks of management by crisis and does not augur well for long-term strategic considerations. The authors offer suggestions about how Africa's existing consultancy resources could be optimally utilized.

In Chapter 15, Fye and Sock provide an insightful analysis of the role of indigenous management consultants in the Gambia's public sector. Their discussion is based mainly on experiences in three government ministries and the country's Management Development Institute. The consultants were hired mainly to advise on structural reorganization of the public service, project planning and implementation, human resources development and utilization, and institutional reform of public enterprises. An increased role of management consultants in the public sector accompanied the advent of a more systematic planned approach to economic management in the mid-1970s.

Fye and Sock give a generally positive assessment of the contribution of indigenous management consultants, who have sometimes worked under conditions and with resources that would have defied the tenacity of the most resilient of non-African consultants. The authors cite cases in which the state employed consultants with sinister motives—for example, to justify predetermined measures or to divert public attention from pressing national problems—as well as cases of local consultants being driven by personal rather than professional motives and, in some cases, deliberately withholding candid advice for fear of touching a raw nerve in government circles. Fye and Sock also cite instances of failure on the part of the Gambian public sector to effectively utilize consultants or their outputs.

The contributions to this volume are priceless because they come from seasoned and highly trained African management consultants with an array of valuable experiences in the profession. They share with the readers some of the instructive and, I dare say, inspiring aspects of their consulting encounters around the continent. The essays draw more upon firsthand field experiences than on published literature. In this lies the unique value of the contributions in the following pages.

Notes

1. Ngure Mwaniki, "Development of Indigenous Consultancy Organizations in Eastern and Southern Africa: A Survey Commissioned by the United Nations Economic Commission for Africa" (unpublished consultancy report prepared for ECA, Addis Ababa, 1979).

2. Paul M. Ndikwe, "Integrated Report of a Mission to Strengthen the Capacity of Indigenous Management Consultants in Nigeria, Ghana, the Gambia, Kenya, Tanzania, Lesotho, Zimbabwe, Zambia and Malawi" (unpublished consultancy report prepared for AAPAM, Addis Ababa, 1989).

3. P. M. Efange and M. Jide Balogun, "Economic Crisis, Organization, and Structure of Government for Recovery and Development: A Comparative Review of Experiences and New Perspectives," in *Economic Restructuring and African Public Administration: Issues, Action and Future Options*, ed. M. Jide Balogun and Gelase Mutahaba (West Hartford, CT: Kumarian Press, 1989), pp. 51–65.

4. Stephen K. Commins, *Africa's Development Challenges and the World Bank: Hard Questions, Costly Choices* (London and Boulder, CO: Lynne Rienner Publishers, 1988), pp. 1–2; Eshetu Chole, "The African Economic Crisis: Origins and Impact on Society," in *Economic Restructuring*, p. 5 ff. For an interesting historical analysis of the external dimension of the crisis, see P. Collier, "Africa's External Economic Relations: 1960–90," *African Affairs* 90 (July 1991):339–56.

5. John Loxley, "The IMF, the World Bank and Sub-Saharan Africa: Policies and Politics," in *The IMF and the World Bank in Africa: Conditionality, Impact and Alternatives*, ed. K. J. Havnevik (Uppsala: Scandinavian Institute of African Studies, 1987), p. 51. See also P. Collier, "Africa's External Economic Relations," and Paul Mosley, "Policy Making Without Facts: A Note on the Assessment of Structural Adjustment Policies in Nigeria, 1985–1990, *African Affairs* 91 (April 1992):227–40; J. Barry Riddell, "Things Fall Apart Again: Adjustment Programs in Sub-Saharan Africa," *Journal of Modern African Studies* 30 (1992):53–68.

6. Loxley, *The IMF*, p. 47 ff.; Efange and Balogun, "Economic Crisis," p. 52.

7. Moses Kiggundu, *Managing Organizations in Developing Countries: An Operational and Strategic Approach* (West Hartford, CT: Kumarian Press, 1989), p. 4.

8. Goran Hyden, *No Shortcuts to Progress: African Development Management in Perspective* (Berkeley and Los Angeles: University of California Press, 1983), ch. 6.

9. Kiggundu, *Managing Organizations*, pp. 7–9.

10. Kiggundu, *Managing Organizations*, p. 149.

11. Kiggundu, *Managing Organizations*, ch. 5.

12. Kiggundu, *Managing Organizations*, ch. 5. See also Paschal B. Mihyo, "The Economic Crisis, Recovery Programmes and Labor in Tanzania," *Labour, Capital and Society* 23 (April 1990):70–99.

13. Ndikwe, *Integrated Report*, p. 6.

14. AAPAM, *Reports of the Workshops for Senior Level Policy Personnel on Optimal Utilization of Management Consultants*, Arusha, Tanzania, 17–21 August 1987, and Accra, Ghana, 22–26 August 1988.

15. See Kwame E. Adjei, "Management Consulting Process: Present Practices and How to Improve Them" (Paper presented to the AAPAM Workshop on Management Consultancy, Arusha, Tanzania, August 1987).

16. Sandile B. Ceko, "Optimal Utilization of Consultants: Swaziland" (Paper presented to the AAPAM Workshop on Management Consultancy, Arusha, Tanzania, August 1987). See also Adjei, "Management Consulting Process."

17. M.K. Consultants, "The Indigenous Consultant's Experience— M.K. Consultants, Tanzania" (Paper presented to the AAPAM Workshop on Management Consultancy, Arusha, Tanzania, August 1987); Professional Training Consultants, "PTC's Experience in Providing Consultancy Services to Various Organizations in Kenya" (Paper presented to the AAPAM Workshop on Management Consultancy, Accra, Ghana, August 1988).

18. Ndikwe, *Integrated Report*, p. 7 ff.

19. Professional Training Consultants, "PTC's Experience"; Mesfin Terrefe, "The Status of Indigenous Management Consultancy in Africa" (Paper presented to the AAPAM Workshop on Management Consultancy, Arusha, Tanzania, August 1987); Maryse Roberts, "Optimal Use of Consultants: Seychelles Experience" (Paper presented to the AAPAM Workshop on Management Consultancy, Arusha, Tanzania, August 1987).

PART I

The African Setting and Context

CHAPTER 1

Issues and Attitudes in Management Consulting

JOSEPH E. KARIUKI

The idea of making greater and more effective use of African consultants and trainers in Africa is not a new one. As far back as June 1974, a joint meeting was organized with the Organization of African Unity (OAU), the Economic Commission for Africa (ECA), the African Development Bank (AfDB), and the African Training and Research Center in Administration for Development (CAFRAD) on the utilization of African experts and resources of technical experience. The discussed issues included the advantages of using indigenous experts, the preparation of a roster of African experts in Africa and abroad, the training of African consultants, reducing and even reversing the African brain-drain trend, the adoption of African intellectual refugees within African states and organizations and making effective use of them in both gainful and beneficial activities, and the financing of some of these activities. This was followed by a distribution of responsibilities among the participating organizations.

As is the case with many other projects in Africa, it is difficult to assess the impact of any of the activities that started as a result of these initiatives. Intra-African projects are often hindered by long distances, communication problems, uncertainty of the tenure in office of prime movers of the projects, shortage of funds to sustain initial efforts, and the constant emergence of new priorities. The list of unresolved practical development problems is long and continues to grow. Recently, while in the process of preparing a paper for another forum, I had an opportunity to look at current literature, some of it originating from the African Association for Public Administration and Management (AAPAM), on African problems and issues. I made the following observation: Given the complexity and the range of issues that African governments have to deal with today, there is simply not enough trained and competent laborpower. A random listing of some of the issues indicates the range of problems:

- *Economic issues:* rural and agricultural development, industrialization, productivity, economic crises, the national debt.

- *Political issues:* bureaucracy, decentralization, political instability, the refugee crisis, national philosophies.

- *Technological issues:* new technology, modernization, shortages of technical expertise.

- *Social and cultural issues:* women's role in development, the impatience of youth, urbanization, educational reform, tribalism, nepotism, corruption, low morale, food shortages, health problems, population problems, illiteracy.

- *International issues:* international trade, multinationals, foreign businesspeople.

Basically there is too much to do by too few who, on the whole, are at the point of giving up.

Most of the issues listed above are not new; they have been with us for a relatively long time. The problem is lack of breakthroughs in finding solutions; there is no sense of having made any real progress. In fact, the evidence is that in Africa as a whole, development efforts have been so disappointing that many argue that the situation is getting worse.

It is, however, easy to fall into the trap of making generalizations. There have been a few cases of positive turnarounds in Africa: in food production, in industrial development, in economic reform, and so on. But they have been too few to have a continental impact. Hence it is frightening to hear leaders declare on public platforms to the international community what great progress has been made since independence while large sections of African society are starving, malnourished, and in ill-health; large sections of some cities are becoming slums; rural underdevelopment persists; the transport sector is declining; and economic neocolonialization is gaining momentum.

The democratic voice of expression is increasingly being muted; the number of refugees is mounting; and the gap between the haves and the have-nots, whether at the African continental level or between the North and the South, is growing. Yet, it has to be admitted that the magnitude of the problems that prevail in specific countries has to be considered relative.

Equally unhelpful are such negative generalizations as statements from so-called intellectuals about the "historic disaster" Africa is headed for. These doomsayers seem as mentally isolated from the dynamics of the real-life operations of public institutions as the leaders they condemn, whether they are viewing the situation from the security of some metropolitan capital or from the insulated cocoon of some university faculty. Those of us who have had the opportunity to meet serious, sincere, hardworking, and committed top-level public servants and leaders operating courageously under severe constraints know that all is not lost and that not every leader is an inveterate "copycat." Yet we have to agree with the intellectuals that the need for change in Africa is urgent and even desperate, and that in many cases "Africa's extreme problems require—dare I say—extreme solutions."[1] Change will require quality leadership that is capable of developing and enunciating meaningful new public policies and plans and a committed cadre of senior performers capable of translating those policies into action programs, implementing them, and evaluating their effectiveness.

In this process of change, which can be executed only by Africans themselves, African experts and consultants must play a vital role. Foreign experts cannot be expected to detach themselves from the basic self-interests of their countries of origin, which have little to do with African development. For developed countries, deeply enmeshed in their own power and political balancing, African development issues remain in the distant periphery of their concerns.

However, going back to the initial efforts aimed at getting Africans to help themselves by using African expertise, we recall that the importance of sharing available expertise among developing countries was stressed by the Lima Declaration. This is completely consonant with the various measures that have been proposed for the promotion of technical cooperation among developing countries.

Stressing the Use of Indigenous Management Consultants

In 1975, CAFRAD organized its first workshop for CAFRAD consultants. This was the beginning of the creation of a network of African consultants and trainers. In the preamble of the aide-mémoire on that network, CAFRAD observed that the gradual awareness of the importance of developing and maintaining a roster of African experts was the result of a number of factors, including:

- Disappointment with some of the Center's non-African consultants because they were either unable to relate to the needs of the clients or uncomfortable handling the high-level participants who attended CAFRAD's meetings;

- CAFRAD's realization that the meetings themselves brought together a wealth of African talent that could be further developed and tapped for the Center's future activities;

- Clear evidence that the African consultants and trainers recruited by CAFRAD provided their services with enthusiasm and genuine involvement in the issues and that their contributions were truly relevant to African problems and realities;

- The fact that, on the whole, African consultants and trainers provided their services at less cost to the Center;

- The enhancement of African consultants' and trainers' own development, which prepared them for further service to Africa;

- The need to make a break with the colonially planted and persistent notion that Africa always had to import skills, ideas, and experience from outside the continent; and

- The importance of promoting both the collective self-reliance of African nations and cooperation among them in the use of available but scarce resources in consulting, training, and research services.

During the workshop one of the workshop groups identified some of the aims of the proposed network as follows:

- To stimulate and mobilize the utilization of African expertise in consultancy in as wide an area as possible;

- To improve the quantity and quality of African expertise in consultancy;

- To promote the professionalization of African consultancy;

- To maintain high standards of professional practice among African consultants;

- To upgrade the status of African consultants on the African continent;

- To encourage the utilization in Africa of African resources residing outside the continent;

- To promote intra-African cooperation in the utilization of available resources; and

- To provide CAFRAD with the capability to generate a flow of consultants, trainers, and researchers.

It would be of great interest to know how the use of the CAFRAD network by African governments and public and other organizations has progressed since this effort was launched.

Since the time when the activities described above were going on, the use of consultancy in Africa has greatly expanded. The initial arguments for greater use of African consultants remain valid and, in many ways, have been strengthened. However, the light in which consulting firms and individuals are viewed has become more complex as more and more administrators and executives experience an increasing number of consulting encounters.

Attitudes toward Foreign Consultants

The desirability, relevance, and competence of foreign consultants' expertise are no longer taken for granted. Some foreign consultants are packaged with various projects offered by donors even when the recipients see no need for particular individuals or when they believe that they have adequate expertise to handle the project in question. Many of the so-called experts have failed to prove themselves in actual performance. These packaging arrangements have therefore been seen as a donor's means of providing employment for its country's nationals, of training its youth for future political or economic exploitation, of directing the project development to suit the interests of the donor, of controlling the use of funds, or even of ensuring that donated funds return to the donor country. When foreign consultants are an inseparable part of a donor's package, they are considered a necessary evil.

There have been cases in which the experts have been rather arrogant and overbearing, have treated assignments as prolonged holiday excursions, and have pursued a life style that took no account of the environment, culture, and material circumstances surrounding them. Such attitudes result in suspicion, hostility, and general resentment against the foreigners.

In industrial circles, foreign consultants are often regarded in the same light as the industries themselves: mainly foreign, promoting foreign interests. When industries are nationalized because of shortages in technical and management skills, foreign experts continue to occupy important positions in the organizations and tend to recommend the recruitment of foreign consultants when specialized services are needed, thus further extending the resentment already generated by their own presence.

The standards of living of foreign experts and consultants are often in such contrast to those of the Africans living around them that it is easy to understand why they are regarded with covert, or even overt, envy. This is especially understandable in the case of local executives and managers who believe that, given a chance, they could be as good as or better than their foreign counterparts. Donors' insistence on the use of their own consultants and experts when local ones are available, and the retention of such experts even after their services are no longer needed, is tantamount to an admission of some of the accusations mentioned above. Such actions amount to a confession that their experts have failed or been unwilling to train their local counterparts.

All this does not imply that technical cooperation is no longer necessary. There are still numerous areas in education, training, and transfer of technology where foreign support is needed. Decisions about which assistance is needed, however, should be made by the leaders of the receiving countries, and they should definitely be involved in the selection of the experts.

Problems Facing African Management Consultants

Various arguments presented earlier should establish the case for using indigenous consultants. One of the most important is the relevance of consultancy in which both the client and the consultant are from the same basic culture; have a common heritage; see themselves as sharing common short-term and longer-term interests in the development of their organizations, their nation, and themselves as individuals; and share a concern for the present welfare of their people and for future generations. Nonetheless, there are still many problems to be overcome before African consultancy, especially in the general management field, can be fully established.

African education has produced acceptable experts and consultants in such professional fields as education, engineering, law, architecture, and medicine as well as in the more technical or functional management areas such as accounting, production, and just recently, management services and computer applications. All these areas involve specialized knowledge that general managers are ready to accept from the appropriate resource persons.

General management, however—involving planning, defining objectives, developing policies, devising strategies, and creating instruments for control and evaluation—is relatively new. Many of the African managers who have made it to the top, especially in public enterprises, acquired their positions through the civil service route or through political intervention rather than from proven business management capability. A few are now being promoted from specialized fields such as engineering. And generally, there are few African managers of major business corporations, since those tend to be foreign. The very few growing African businesses are the products of industrial entrepreneurs.

Under these circumstances, there are few examples of local managerial excellence to speak of. On the one hand, individual African enterprises are still rather young and on the whole small scale; on the other hand, most large public enterprises have not been great examples of excellence so far. Management consultants have to deal with predominantly practical managers in the context of suggesting interventions intended to bring about performance improvement. Since there is so little excellence in the recent brief history of African-managed organizations, where would such African consultants come from? If they come from successful foreign businesses, they are likely to be too young to have reached top management levels. Those who do reach top levels tend to stay because of the good opportunities and conditions of corporate service. Other possible sources of consultants are the universities. But their expertise is likely to be suspect, sometimes with justification, since they have had little or no experience in the world of work. It is common knowledge that some persons with advanced degrees in public administration have made poor administrators or managers when put to the test within organizations. In the Western world, grave doubts have been raised regarding the suitability of traditional university teaching of business management.

It is to be expected, then, that new African managers with little experience themselves in business management will doubt whether local consultants can truly help them improve the performance of their organizations. They would rather turn to foreign consultants whom they can associate with the success of other enterprises.

The managers themselves, being unsure of their own competence to handle this whole new area, are not so keen to expose their shortcomings to outsiders, especially to other Africans. Traditionally, it has been accepted as normal to learn from Europeans: they come from an "advanced" cultural background. An African manager might say to himself, "What has a chap from my village, who walked barefooted just the other day, who may be even younger than I and less experienced in life, have to offer me with my status and public recognition? What will people think if they thought I was learning anything from him at my age?"

Some of the older generation suffer from colonial hang-ups and other out-of-date conceptions. They simply do not believe that Africans can do a better job than the white man. They do not make decisions because they are afraid of "the boss," even though they are now the bosses—not some white men who left when they took over. They will not delegate because they are afraid of bright young people. They will not have an African consultant who threatens to turn things upside down. Such people surely should not be in managerial positions. There will be little progress while they are still around. They may have been appointed because they were nice and safe, but they are no longer relevant to development. Progressive management involves innovation, accepting the need for change, managing that change, making decisions, and taking calculated risks. They will be afraid of any form of consultancy because it will most likely introduce some newfangled ideas bound to rock the boat.

Another problem facing African management consulting efforts is the fact that consultants charge relatively high fees. They have a valuable service to offer at a price, but a manager has to be able to justify the cost. When a transaction requires a document from a lawyer or an accountant, the manager has no choice but to pay. However, when it is a matter of general improvement of performance, even when it is clear that the organization is ailing, many African managers would rather wait and see, hope that things improve, that they will muddle through. Besides, having to pay fees that managers themselves cannot command—and to another African—becomes a painful personal rather than organizational issue. It is less painful if some donor agency has to pay, although even that can cause some level of jealousy. It is worse still when managers believe that they could do the job as well or better if they only had the time to put the information together, do an analysis, and write up the findings themselves. But the fact is that as long as they are doing their present job, they will never be in a position to do that. They may try to get some members of their team to do the job, and they will give it their best efforts, but interruptions from routine work will lead to an unsatisfactory and inconclusive hodgepodge.

The circumstances described above imply that African management consultants have a difficult time convincing managers to have confidence in their ability. They are denied opportunities to perform and consequently to develop their skills and gain the experience they need to do a better job. They get caught in a vicious circle that may lead to insecurity and uncertainty about the future, loss of self-confidence, stress, poor performance, poor earnings, and weak negotiating positions, since they have no tangible evidence of effective past performance. As they say, nothing succeeds like success. Managers are unwilling to stake their investments on someone with a dubious track record.

The safest African consultants are those in specialized fields and those who are attached to well-established foreign consulting firms and international multilateral organizations. Some of them, however, tend to become overconfident and develop an inflated sense of their own worth. Sometimes they begin to lose sight of their organizations' mission and the need for tact in providing services, thus giving their organizations and themselves a bad name. I have often heard complaints like: "These UN chaps with their fat salaries think that they can bully us in our own country. Who do they think they are? Some of them are useless and do nothing anyway. We'll show them who's the boss here! After all, look at the country where so-and-so comes from. I've been there. They have nothing to teach us."

One final problem regarding African consultants' efforts to sell their services relates to shortages in new technology, financing projects, and foreign exchange. As a result, consultants cannot package their work in a form that is competitive. This may give the impression of shoddiness or lack of professionalism and prove to be an unfair detraction in otherwise good work. Other elements such as poor machines and paper and lack of secretarial and administrative support can also be major handicaps, not to mention having to operate in a foreign language.

Developing the Consulting Profession in Africa

In spite of everything, progress in making use of African expertise is definitely being made, with some African regional and subregional organizations providing excellent leadership. The UN agencies, the World Bank, and the Commonwealth Fund for Technical Cooperation have been recruiting Africans to serve in projects and in regional and national offices for quite a while. In my opinion, not enough has been done, but a useful beginning has been made. Much more must be done to promote this trend, especially at the national level.

It comes as a surprise to many senior managers and administrators when one of their employees, who has been given little recognition at home, suddenly leaves employment to join an international organization. Such employees sometimes come back to provide high-priced services in their areas of expertise to their former organizations. The lesson to be learned by Africans in senior positions is that they have among their staffs talented and capable performers who must be utilized more effectively, both in their organizations and at the national level. Further, leaders must encourage the idea of searching for talent at home before looking elsewhere for consultants.

Training

Now that the number of African consulting firms and individual consultants is increasing (more so in some African countries than in others), one of the first things that must be intensified is the training and development of consultants. To become a consultant, one has to have the right qualities. The International Labor Organization (ILO) guide to the profession, *Management Consulting,* indicates some of the necessary intellectual, personal, and other qualities under the following headings:

- Intellectual ability.

- Ability to understand people and work with them.

- Ability to communicate, persuade, and motivate.

- Intellectual and emotional maturity.

- Personal drive and initiative.

- Ethics and integrity.

- Physical and mental health.

Assuming that the potential consultant has the relevant qualities, there are still skills that can be learned to ensure that the consultant has the "ability and confidence to carry out assignments in his field of management; investigate an existing situation and design improvements; develop a collaborative relationship with the client; gain acceptance of the proposed changes and implement change satisfactorily; develop proficiency in his field or discipline; satisfy the management of the consulting organization that he is capable of working independently and under pressure to the required standard."

The areas to be covered in initial training fall under the following headings:

- Orientation to management consulting.

- Overview of the consulting process.

- Consulting skills I: Analytical and problem solving.

- Consulting skills II: Behavioral and communication.

- Consulting skills III: Marketing and managing assignments.

- Managing and developing a consulting organization.

Although the most important part of a consultant's training is practical participation in actual consulting work, there are certain skills that can and should be imparted at an early stage. These skills will enable the aspiring consultant to proceed with confidence in a field that has tended to be clouded with an aura of mystery. The training issue is stressed here because, to my knowledge, there is very little organized training for consultants being offered in Africa. Most African consultants made the decision to enter the field and then learned as they went along. AAPAM might consider the recent workshops it organized as the a first step toward meeting the training challenge and work with other regional and subregional organizations to fill the gap.

Consultant-Client Relationships

Assuming that a management consultant has managed to break through the barriers indicated above and enter the profession, what kind of consultant-client relationship will facilitate achievement of their mutual objectives?

In my experience—both as someone who has used the services of consultants and as a consultant myself—I have found that the best relationship is one in which the two parties really work together. As a manager, I wanted to know that my consultant clearly understood my perception of the problem. I was prepared to spend a considerable amount of time up-front to get my point across regarding the problem and my vision of where we wanted to go. Then I listened carefully to the consultant's feedback to make sure that before any serious work started, we truly understood each other and were talking about the same things. Once this was established, I made it clear to all the other parties concerned, who were already in the picture, that they should provide the consultant with all the necessary support. At this point, I normally felt comfortable leaving the consultant to get on with the job, with minimal updates related to progress being made, until a draft report was prepared. Then I felt the need, once again, to spend a good deal of time scrutinizing the report, asking questions, and ensuring that we totally agreed on what was to go into the final report.

As a consultant, I have found it useful after initial discussions, especially when the terms of reference for the assignment are not clearly spelled out, to prepare notes on my understanding of what is to be done, usually in a format that resembles what I expect the terms of reference to look like (without actually saying so). Then I ask the client to correct any misunderstandings and request the client to provide the formal terms of reference. Quite often this facilitates the client's preparation of the terms of reference; my understanding of the needs often come back to me as terms of reference with little alteration. If this initial agreement is reached, not much can go wrong after that. The client and the consultant are on the same track from the start and should reach the desired goals together.

How closely the consultant and client work together throughout the consultancy depends on the nature of the problem and the kind of client. In some cases, the problem is defined jointly and then the consultant is left alone to get on with the job, with only the necessary progress reviews and consultations. Sometimes a problem is defined and the consultant is expected to produce the final answer. This is possible if the consultant is a specialist dealing with a problem with a more or less closed-ended solution.

When dealing with a situation that demands some basic change, it is most important that the client truly knows the problem. The client's team should analyze the problem, explore alternative solutions, decide on the best practical solution, implement the change process, and control and review the results. In this case the consultant is basically a catalyst, providing "how to do it" rather than "what to do" advice. The point is that whatever change is decided on must come from the client system, because the clients have to live with that change. They will do so only if they believe that the change is good for them and have made a commitment to implement the change.

A successful working relationship requires that consultants be able to listen without prejudging the situation; have empathy and be able to identify with the client's problems; be flexible enough to adjust to the client's environment, including the client's culture, tradition, habits, and expression; and be objective and sincere when taking a strong position (from the inside). Consultants must be perceived as wishing the organization and its team the best in terms of improvement in performance. They must not be suspected of hiding the tricks of their trade or of seeing themselves as magicians who know all and can perform wonders. Finally, consultants must be encouraging and supportive without, of course, accepting anything that might compromise their integrity. An atmosphere of mutual trust and openness must be established.

Consultants must always remember that they are dealing with intelligent people who know their problems and what they would like to see happen if they had an ideal situation; but they are hampered by their own environment and sometimes bureaucracy. They need input that encourages them to believe that they can solve their own problems and confirmation that their own intelligent hunches are correct and realistic. They may also need the professional authority of the consultant to back them up, especially if their superiors are unreceptive to their suggestions.

Most of the above is possible if the client is progressive and truly wants change. Such a position facilitates the consultants' entry into the organization and their eventual acceptance as a member of the team. But this is not always the case. For example, a consultant may be hired because a senior manager is dissatisfied with the performance of a particular unit. The consultant may find himself dealing with a hostile group of employees in that unit. The leader of the unit may be the real problem, but for some reason management has been reluctant to remove him, especially if he has political connections. The consultant may discover all this too late and find himself in real trouble. Information will be hidden from him. Administrative support, transport, and secretarial services may be denied. In this case, he has to do the best he can, produce his report, and quit, leaving the authorities who appointed him to do whatever they want. In all likelihood, they only wanted the information they already had confirmed by a neutral source, providing them with the necessary ammunition to take drastic action.

Sometimes the client group is hostile because of unfortunate experiences with other consultants. In one case, a consultant was hired to produce a project document after attempts by two other consultants had already been rejected and the client's own effort had not been accepted by the donor, although the basic principles of the project had been agreed on and the funds had been allocated but not released. The main fault was that the efforts by the previous consultants had not seriously considered the client's position; the consultants had assumed that they understood, from the terms of reference, what the client needed. Further, there were hints in the document that the client was ineffective and that the consultants did not respect the efforts going on in the unit. Moreover, the job description for the project manager perfectly fitted one of the consultants, which made the intentions of their work most suspicious. The client's effort had been rejected by the donor because it was too long and did not conform to the standard format.

The new consultant found the client in a very unhappy mood and generally ready to attack any consultant's proposals. During a two-month assignment, it took a whole month before the consultant was properly introduced to the group as a whole. The consultant spent the first month looking at whatever documents she could lay her hands on (they were not always easy to come by) and gently trying to develop a communication base with the team. Since most of the necessary information was there, she decided that this was basically a human relations problem.

To cut a long story short, once the new consultant was accepted, it took only a week to produce a rough draft. This was ruthlessly scrutinized by the group, and she kept on producing revised versions. The fifth version was no longer her document; it was the group's document, but it was more concise, had eliminated previous criticisms of the group, and was in the format the donor required. The assignment was over. The consultant made sure that the duration of the contract of the proposed project manager was reduced and refused to write the job description, since the group knew exactly the kind of expert it needed. The project document was accepted by all the parties concerned.

There are many examples of what can go wrong. It seems to me, however, that a consultant has to start by being aware of potential problems, look out for them from the beginning, identify them, and decide on how to cope with them before plunging into the substantive elements. This is particularly important in process consulting. Second, consultants must respect the people they are dealing and working with; only then can they gain respect and achieve the necessary climate of mutual trust. Last, consultants must remember that they are only short-term guests in the organization—that the problems of the organization belong to the client, as do the solutions. It should be clear that they recognize and respect that ownership.

As indicated at the beginning, there are numerous problems and issues in Africa, and we need all the local expertise we can muster. AAPAM's efforts in promoting the cause of optimal utilization of African consultants is most timely and welcome. It should be supported, intensified, and, to the extent possible, decentralized (while retaining AAPAM's leadership), so that it can reach as many parts of Africa as possible.

Note

1. Kofi Buenor Hadjor, *On Transforming Africa—Discourse with African Leaders* (Trenton, NJ: African World Press, 1987), p. 6.

CHAPTER 2

The State of Management
Consulting in Africa

NGURE MWANIKI

There are many reasons for cherishing, supporting, and promoting local or indigenous consultancy firms and organizations in Africa. Some of these reasons are generally accepted and hardly debatable, such as the following:

- Africa consumes large amounts of foreign exchange in the employment of foreign consultants, which not only drains development resources from the continent but also creates unemployment of equally qualified local consultants.

- Indigenous consultancy firms could become equally, if not more, competitive with their foreign counterparts if they were offered local management consulting opportunities. Given their intimate knowledge of the local environment, indigenous consultants are better placed to adapt available management knowledge to specific local conditions.

- Local consultancy firms would be better able to organize themselves and operate on a cooperative basis, which is necessary if they are to become more effective, given the constraints and the changing environment in which they operate.

- Local consultancy skills, in combination with those from overseas, would provide the best results—blending local and international experience into one component.

For our purposes, indigenous management consulting firms can be defined as those whose ownership and control, in terms of shareholding and management, are more than 50 percent indigenous. Three key measures of control are (1) African shareholding, (2) the proportion of African professional staff, and (3) the extent of actual management control by Africans.

At the local level, the course of economic growth and development in each African country has created an increase in the utilization of consultancy services in general and local services in particular. However, the use of consultants is influenced by constraints on public and private investment and the process of economic change in general. Prominent among such constraints is scarcity of development resources.

The local consulting effort can be measured by the existence of identifiable consulting organizations, institutions, and firms as well as by individuals who offer consulting services to both public and private sectors, depending on their areas of competence and specialization. Some of the more common areas of specialization within African management consulting firms are:

- Engineering

- Research and training

- Development economics and management

- Advertising and public relations

- Data processing

- Architecture and surveying

- Agroindustrial and rural integrated development studies

- Business management, growth, and development economics

Specializations and fields of competence vary from country to country, given the diversity of natural resources endowment and levels of economic growth and development. However, the professional growth of local management consulting throughout Africa has been affected by certain specific problems and constraints pertaining to how local consultants acquire the necessary skills, competence, and higher levels of specialization.

Given that most African professionals in the management consulting field obtained their skills abroad, their biggest challenge is to adapt that knowledge and professional competence to their own local conditions. Despite the efforts of the African Training and Research Center in Administration for Development (CAFRAD) and the African Association for Public Administration and Management (AAPAM) on this front, there is still a lot to be done. There must be a concerted effort by all the relevant parties: policymakers, public and private institutions, and individual professionals. The latest effort by AAPAM to organize workshops and other activities aimed at enhancing African indigenous management consultancy capacity and capability is of utmost importance. It has great potential for the development of African management consultancy resources.

In 1978, the Economic Commission for Africa (ECA) surveys covering eastern, southern and central Africa established the number of indigenous consultancy firms as follows:[1]

Kenya, 4

Tanzania, 10

Uganda, 10

Zambia, 5

Botswana, 2

Lesotho, 3

Mauritius, 2

Seychelles, 1

Zaire, 9

Gabon, 1

Congo, 3

Cameroon, 11

Owing to the lack of more recent and comprehensive surveys, it is difficult to quantify the increase and growth of indigenous consulting firms. There is no doubt, however, that these firms have experienced recent rapid growth, for a variety of reasons. Chief among them is the increased rate of economic growth and development in a number of African countries. In addition, the growth in the number of institutions of higher learning within Africa itself has provided greater opportunities for higher education, increasing indigenous knowledge and skills.

The growth of indigenous consulting firms can also be attributed to the increase in the amount of local skills and expertise available. The civil service, which in many countries had a monopoly on the most qualified people, has declined as the main employer of these professionals (at least, this appears to be the case). Although the public sector still remains a major employer of skilled local resources, the private sector has recently acquired increasing importance and plays a greater role in the employment of local consultants, especially in the accounting and financial services fields.

Development agencies such as the African Development Bank (AfDB), the ECA, the World Bank, and the U.S. Agency for International Development (USAID) have also played significant roles in recognizing African management consultants. In fact, the African Development Bank provides a secretariat for one of the more active associations of African management consultants.

Problems of African Management Consulting Firms

Management consultancy in developing countries has been slow, relative to consulting in other fields such as accounting, architecture, and engineering.[2] This phenomenon can be attributed in part to the widespread lack of organization and focus on the part of local management consultants.[3] This weakness is often manifested in the inability to meet the diverse needs of project development and management, largely due to a failure to share information, personnel, and skills and to cooperate and associate in ways that economize scarce resources.

As it stands today, many project management assignments are beyond the capabilities of the small units of local management consultants. The combination of problems and constraints faced by local consultants has created an environment in which institutions and enterprises in the developing countries themselves tend to prefer foreign consultants for their more significant projects. The consequence is that foreign consulting firms have now claimed Africa as a serious export market for their skills. African institutions have therefore inadvertently helped to reinforce the belief that management consulting is the domain of foreign consultants and that local consultants are not quite as accomplished. And the practices of some local management consultants have done little to alleviate this negative attitude.

A list of complaints from local management consulting firms about their problems, constraints, and frustrations in their areas of operation would be lengthy—if not endless—due to the diversity of operational, institutional, political, social, and ethical matters facing these firms. However, eight specific problems can be identified.

The first is lack of acceptance. Acceptance and confidence can be achieved only if local consultants are allowed to demonstrate their usefulness. In the African context, where management consulting is a relatively new discipline, many policymakers and top managers still need to be persuaded of the potential benefits of management consultancy. It is crucial that they be convinced of the need for and benefits of consultancy services, especially at critical times of financial or managerial crises, when they need the services most, as well as on a long-term basis.

The second problem is the dearth of trained labor. Improvement of management consulting skills, especially specialized skills, is a major objective that decisionmakers and consultants should pursue together for mutual benefit. Specific problems in this area include a serious workforce deficiency in management consulting, lack of qualified staff in the technical fields, lack of institutional facilities, and shortage of specialized personnel.

The third problem has to do with relations of economic dependence between rich and poor countries. The effects of this relationship on local management consultants is probably best summarized in the unpalatable phrase, "beggars can't be choosers." In many countries, acceptance of grants for consultancy studies means that the donor provides the consultants.

The fourth constraint relates to culture. A good example of how culture inhibits African management consultants is the generation gap. The generation gap often inhibits older, more experienced African managers, decisionmakers, and administrators from listening to advice given by younger professionals who have not yet made it big, and definitely cannot claim to have the wisdom of ages.

Fifth is the issue of policy, which includes all the complaints relating to unfair competition, lack of policy support, various malpractices, and lack of clear guidelines and procedures. Clear policy guidelines would reduce conflicts. Competition, an otherwise healthy component of growth in any profession, is positive only when it is fair.

A related sixth problem is institutional. The weaknesses of the local consulting firms render them unable to compete with their foreign counterparts. Growth of the profession should be accompanied by better organization. This goes hand in hand with policy support.

A seventh set of problems pertains to ethical issues. These permeate some of the other considerations but are at the heart of the standards that must be established in the course of growth of the management consulting profession. They include social behavior, integrity, technical and professional competence, and standards of performance. But ethical standards involve the responsibility of the client as well, especially when it comes to payment for services rendered.

Last are the behavioral aspects that adversely affect the consulting environment. These relate to a range of negative attitudes of potential clients toward local management consultants and include prejudice, mistrust, and preconceived judgment. This category of complaints consists of both individual and social behavior and is most difficult to rectify.

All these problems interplay collectively and simultaneously to determine the present status of indigenous management consulting in African countries. Of course, different local firms in different countries and regions are affected to varying degrees by varying environmental factors. But the general characteristic feature of local management consultancy services remains the stiff competition from more powerful foreign firms. In the eyes of a prospective client who, more often than not, commands both political influence and financial resources, foreign consultancy firms are more knowledgeable and more experienced. This lack of acceptance of local consulting firms, coupled with their poor resource base in terms of capital, qualified personnel, financing, materials, and equipment, tends to constrain their development.

Agenda for Action

Training

Training is essential in order to combat the lack of technical knowledge and expertise in the various areas of specialization and competence. Due to the complexity of the management problems faced in developing countries, training programs for management consultants must be diversified, tapping all possible training opportunities—both formal and on the job. Training programs should also prepare the would-be consultants for the realities and complexities of development management as well as teach them how to adapt their technical and managerial know-how to the prevailing local environment.

In the short run, local consultants should be given opportunities to participate in practical management consultancy assignments in development programs and projects in their own countries, regions, and subregions. Such opportunities exist within such development institutions as ECA, the African Development Bank, the World Bank, and others. Such involvement would enable them to gain not only professional competence but also greater insights into the realities of local management consulting. It would also provide a stimulus for them to aim for excellence in the profession.

In the long run, training and development of the workforce must be reinforced by the utilization of indigenous management consultants. Various African governments have already come out with major policy statements on the use of local consultants, but the full realization of these policies depends on the actions that follow the pronouncements.

Government Policy

Government support is crucial. Institutional strengthening can occur only when local firms enjoy considerable policy support, which is also a precondition for the growth and development of the profession. A serious conflict between government and the business sector about the role of local consulting organizations would adversely affect the climate conducive to the growth of the consulting profession. A typically favorable policy framework that supports management consultants includes such measures as:

1. Promoting legislation that would facilitate the establishment and operation of local consulting services;

2. Applying fair policies for remunerating local consultants;

3. Encouraging the involvement of local consultants in assignments that are managed by more experienced foreign consultants;

4. Removing any other policies that might discriminate against less experienced, though basically competent, local management consultants—be they firms or individuals; and

5. Evaluating local consultants' services objectively without accepting low-quality service just for the sake of localization.

Donor Agencies

Consulting assignments in the developing countries of Africa and elsewhere are financed largely through technical assistance packages comprising loans and grants for specific development projects and programs. At present, donor agencies are the major financiers of consultancy services in Africa, usually for governments and the public sector in general. Therefore, their support is crucial; they must be persuaded to involve local consultants in the consultancy assignments they sponsor.

Joint Ventures

Joint ventures provide both a healthy environment for consulting work and learning opportunities for emerging local consultants. The blending of local and international skills, knowledge, and experience in the field of management consulting yields mutually beneficial results. The local consultant can take advantage of the long and varied experiences of other consulting institutions operating globally. The foreign firm gains deeper insights into the problem at hand by teaming up with local professionals who have intimate knowledge of the environment and culture. One practical program for improving the technical competence of African consultants is to require foreign firms to have local counterparts in bidding for and carrying out consultancy assignments.

Associations

Interaction with other entities involved in management consulting goes a long way in the enhancement of consulting capacity. As the profession grows, it needs to organize itself into associations, which can play a useful role in promoting standards and safeguarding ethics. Management consultants would also be better able to confront the wide range of problems discussed above if they worked together. Associations would also facilitate the gaining of government support and enhance the consulting profession's collective bargaining power in pursuit of its common interests and demands. Also, firms could pool scarce skills and resources and share facilities such as data processing and printing.

Code of Ethics for African Consultants

A code of ethics is needed to enhance professional standards. Professional standards pertain to competence, integrity, and performance with respect to the services offered to clients. A code of ethics takes a collection of norms and principles and raises it to the art and practice of a profession.

One of the basic ethical issues in management consulting is confidentiality of client information. Lack of such confidentiality will constrain the amount of information managers are willing to reveal to outside consultants.

A consultant should never take advantage of a client's inexperience in dealing with consultants and using their services. It is the consultant's responsibility to enlighten the client about the nature of the consultant-client relationship and even to provide advice on the optimal utilization of the consultant's skills and resources.

A consultant must never misrepresent himself or herself to a client, mislead, or unduly and consciously influence a client's choice, supervision, or evaluation of a consultant and the consulting services rendered. Self-discipline is imperative. Observation of agreed-on time schedules and deadlines for accomplishment of assignments is crucial to success.

Clients must also have ethical standards. Most important, a client must attach sufficient value to the consultancy offered. If client behavior indicates otherwise, the assignment should be suspended. This is a warning that the client may not honor the contract and may withhold payment for services rendered. If the client is not the paying party, the effort is futile and a waste of resources, since an uninterested client is unlikely to implement a consultant's recommendations.

The client's choice of a consultant should not be based on ambiguous and dubious criteria but strictly on technical competence and economic efficiency. This reduces the chance of future dishonesty, refusal to pay, delays in payment, or disappointment in either the consultant or the services provided.

Adherence to a code of ethics is very important if the profession is to gain its due respect from donor agencies, the professional international community, local governments, and clients. Work ethics have to be observed and quality maintained. Consultants should not accept payment for work that was not done. Also, the utility of the end product must be closely linked to the development process. This means that the product of the consulting effort must be in a form that can be used by policy- and decisionmakers.

Notes

1. Surveys by N. Mwaniki and E. Metuge, ECA consultant experts (1978).

2. ECA surveys (1978).

3. Milan Kubr, ed., *Management Consulting: A Guide to the Profession,* 2d rev. ed. (Geneva: International Labor Organization, 1986).

CHAPTER 3

The Origins and Future
of African Consulting

G. C. M. MUTISO

In the aide-mémoire for the workshops that preceded publication of this book, the African Association for Public Administration and Management (AAPAM) stated that the workshops were "aimed at enhancing the optimal utilization of the [consulting] resources that are already available." In this spirit, rather than narrate the trials and tribulations of building a small African consulting firm, this chapter dwells on the traditions of consulting that influence our thinking about consulting on this continent.

African consulting borrows heavily from, and in some respects is held hostage by, traditions developed elsewhere. As a result, it has not developed a coherent professional focus, for there are strong forces aligned against it that stem primarily from borrowed traditions and the continents' sociopolitical circumstances. This chapter deals extensively with these borrowed traditions, for they are often ignored when we think of the growth of this sector.

The External Engineer Tradition

Consulting firms that are not in the engineering sciences are a recent phenomenon even in the developed world. There the first consulting firms were engineering firms that arose out of the industrial need to locate and design the equipment necessary to exploit raw materials. The tradition of the importance of outside consultants grew out of the belief that the consultants knew something the owners did not. As holders of specialized information that was beyond the reach of the owners, consultants became important actors in the growth of production in mining-type industries.

It is clear that in the developed world the growth of the engineering profession and the organization of engineers into consulting groups were significant in the expansion of raw material production. The engineers became prestigious as they initially located resources and then developed the industrial methods for processing them by either individual entrepreneurs or companies.

African engineers have not been tied to production. First, the economies of the countries are directed mainly by foreigners, and raw materials are shipped out. Second, African engineers have not tried to develop their own production/design or ownership niche because they do not understand how critical their profession is in the growth of production in the industrialized world. They have not used their skills to become entrepreneurs in a continent that is crying out for entrepreneurship based on our exploitation of our own resources for industrialization. Most, whether they work for the dominant multinational consulting firms or African firms, still function as technicians drawing what state bureaucracies order. We on the African continent need to put these technical minds into production, ownership, and design positions if we are to have any chance of controlling and increasing the rate of our own development based on the resources on this continent.

Such a niche is already seen as important by the immigrant communities in Africa, which invest heavily in engineering training. These communities use the outputs of that training for production and managerial purposes in the technical fields. The long-term implications are that the key production and technical fields will continue to be monopolized by the immigrant communities. African states need to realize this and to understand that society will eventually rebel against this foreign control, as it rebelled against colonialism.

The External Economist Tradition

Since World War II, a new type of consultant-specialist in the social sciences has emerged, particularly in the United States—an economist created by the large-scale planning that was undertaken during the war. However, it is important to underscore the point that those who came to the fore in the consulting world and made an impact on the development of the sector were propelled by a kind of sociopolitical activism that pushed public institutions and policy into areas that had been ignored.

The role of consulting firms in desegregation cases and foreign aid activities in the 1950s is unique. Such firms were able to move into research and documentation of social phenomena that the conventional institutions of knowledge—universities and foundations—dared not touch, for they were too tied to the biases of the time.

Significant in the growth of foreign aid was the contribution of the consulting firms that pioneered economic notions of how to design and manage development projects. Some of them became so arrogant and dominant in their prescriptions that they continue to shape the teaching of project management to key aid donors, nongovernmental organizations (NGOs), and Third World governments, in spite of the fact that their hidebound economic systems have been shown to be antithetical to world development, not just Third World development.

Indeed, it may well be that the problem of inappropriate development aid is traceable to the dominance of economic consulting firms and the fact that many governments, universities, banks, NGOs, and foundations in the developed world have aped their theories of what should be done in the Third World. They bear the main responsibility for perpetuating an irrelevant advisory system to donors and recipients. They continue to succeed in this because they recruit from the ranks of retirees from both donor and recipient organizations, offering attractive remuneration. Such "inbreeding" ensures that no new blood is introduced that may question their operations. It assures that no new directions are charted.

The External Accountant Tradition

When companies were owned by single persons, the bookkeeper was an ordinary employee who followed the owner's instructions. This was the pattern during Western industrialization through the arrival of corporations in the late nineteenth and early twentieth centuries. However, with the management revolution—when financial whiz kids got to be managers of large scale corporations—accountants graduated from the bookkeeper role.

In some ways this transformation correlates with the changing needs of multinational corporations. They required accountants who were familiar with myriad currency transactions rather than mere bookkeepers.

This change speedily spilled over into the accounting profession, and small accounting firms became multinational. We thus have the current situation of some of the world's accounting being done by multinational accounting firms.

Central to the notion of bookkeeping was the idea of watching over pennies. Bookkeepers therefore advised owners of the pitfalls of investing pennies as well as advising them about greener pastures. This also became the tradition of accountants as they moved up to become financial advisers to large corporations. However, as large accounting firms multinationalized, they found that they were not earning as much money from regular accounting work as they were from management advising, so they created management advisory services as distinct business units. These units were not rooted in any discipline. They functioned like the proverbial witch doctor who throws everything into the pot, for the message is the brew!

These new units fed on the accounting functions. As the accountants went about their business, they spied on other needs and recommended their management colleagues to come marching in soon after.

This practice is well developed on the African continent. Our public officials either do not know enough about it or do not see anything wrong with it. It is said that the major British accounting and management firms get most of their income from Africa.

The creation of management components in accounting firms has led to serious problems for large corporations as well as governments in the North. The essence of the matter is conflict of interests. The question being asked by governments and corporations is: How can someone provide advice on what to do and then turn around and watch over the pennies? Such pressures have led the accounting profession in countries such as Britain into direct clashes with the state and the private sector. There are pressures for such firms to corporately separate accounting and audit services from management advisory services. In Kenya and probably in some other African countries, such issues are discussed by the profession behind closed doors. The issue is not yet on the public plate.

The Peculiar Roots and Grafts

The roots of African consulting were formed in the 1970s after the first decade of independence. There are essentially three reasons for this. First is the labor constraint brought about by the colonial inheritance. There were simply not enough Africans qualified to fill the public and private sectors and spill over into consulting. The second reason is that African consulting attracts a particular type of individual—essentially those who are not attracted to routine or to public roles in the limelight. Third, there was no market for consultants during the first decade of independence. African governments did not, and still do not, go out of their way to support the emergence of African consultants. This last point is important, for one of the peculiarities of African consulting is that it seems to have grown where a peculiar mix of public, nongovernmental, donor, and private-sector activities in the economy facilitated its role. The consultants had to exist in the marketplace on their own before the state found a use for them. This seems to be the case in Egypt, Nigeria, and Kenya.

This peculiar mix, as it applied to Kenya, is the focus of the balance of this chapter. It documents the continuing domination of the sector by foreign firms.

Kenya Accounting Firms: The First Two Decades

A careful look into the consulting scene in Kenya shows that there was a plethora of small British- and Asian-owned accounting firms at independence. With the initial panic after independence, most individual British accountants in Kenya sold out to large firms, usually becoming partners in the new creations. The new firms were able to get a few of the new politically important Africans to act on their behalf in the state arena, particularly by getting them parastatal and ministry work. By the 1970s, the number of local firms had been consolidated through buyouts by large British accounting multinationals. By the mid-1980s, one of the score of companies that dominated the field was negotiating to sell out to a large American multinational. This may be a good indicator of the private- and public-sector shift from British to American primacy.

The Asian individual firms also consolidated during the first decade. However, they were more resilient than the small British firms to takeover pressures because many were supported through a network of religious communities. A few of the smaller ones sold out to the British firms. Some closed shop and went into trade.

The large British firms had begun to bring in junior African accountants in the late 1960s by raiding the public sector. Because there was a great shortage of African accountants at independence—a shortage that some will argue is still with us because of the professional bodies' restrictions on entry—there was a scramble for those Africans who had qualified early, entered the public sector, and moved up. Many public-sector accountants were recruited by accounting firms, and they usually left the public sector having negotiated transfer of the accounting and audit work to their new multinational employers.

Initially, the accountants saw nothing wrong with their recruitment to these companies, but as the 1980s passed and the ownership opportunities they had been promised evaporated, they began to agitate against the multinationals' penetration of the nation's public affairs. A few have quit the multinationals and are scrambling to set up their own companies. Since they are masters at leaving with work, some are wounding the multinationals by taking major clients with them. Since their primary purpose within the multinationals was to liaise with other Africans within the public sector, their exit also creates problems of access. And yet they are not the key players in the long term. In my opinion, the ones to watch are the young Africans who have created small but very aggressive companies and are expanding the service into sectors the profession has ignored.

Transformation of Accounting Firms to Management Firms

In Kenya, management consulting was generated, and continues to be dominated, by British multinational accounting firms that initially fed on the parastatals and ministries. Asian firms did not move into management consulting because the growth of the private sector, which their communities control, provides more than adequate work.

The business practice of the British multinationals was to use their employees to identify management needs as they fulfilled the historical role of accounting. And, of course, they had an accounting monopoly since they and their antecedents were the only firms at independence. In their quest for domination of the management consulting sector, they found natural allies among the bilateral, multilateral, and NGO donors by arguing that their work standards were Western. So much for professionalism!

The few African accountants who set up their own accounting firms before the 1980s, usually as a reaction against fronting for foreign firms and not getting the benefits, had to compete ruthlessly with the large British companies. More often than not they were left to service the minor African business sector and the cooperatives. The accounting and management needs of all donor agencies, NGOs, and multinational firms were fulfilled by the large British accounting multinationals through the 1970s. This practice was basically donor driven, because the donors insisted that the accounting multinationals watch over their money, projects, and programs.

The few African-owned firms did not stand a chance of influencing the sector's orientation and thus contributing to the generation of relevant development. Therefore the ideology of development articulated by the sector was conventional. There was very little work coming out of it that addressed the now known needs of appropriate development for the country. The problem is simply that the consulting sector functions under a historical role assumption that began with the external accountant tradition: Give me the figures, and you will get your accounts.

When management firms are supposed to be creative and give problem-solving development advice, they cannot transcend their discipline, cultural, and maybe parent state orientations. More significantly, the accounting multinationals are no longer the architects of the access game.

Local consulting firms are increasingly mastering that game, and the sociopolitical processes increasingly favor nationals. This, the multinationals' Achilles heel, has created a niche for indigenous firms to grow in the 1990s.

Mutations in Future Growth

The late 1970s saw a motley of Africans creating their firms in Kenya. Some were first-generation bureaucrats who arrived by way of multinational firms. Some were young bureaucrats disillusioned by the perils of public service or bypassed for promotion because of their ethnic affiliation. Others were academics seeking better incomes. Many were graduates who could not find work in other sectors. A few came out of the NGO sector. All have done varied work. If all the engineering, accounting, management, architectural, agricultural, economic, training, and planning consulting firms registered as owned by Africans are added up, they total about 500. Since there is no formal study of the sector (something AAPAM could assist in), it is difficult to state definitively what they do and what experiences they have accumulated.

African firms are convinced that they could have done better if the state had had a different attitude.

First, the state could have assisted them financially by giving soft loans to facilitate purchase of production equipment and operating overdrafts or performance bonds. Setting up a modern firm is expensive, and since it is a service as well as a business, many believe that the state should treat the sector the same way that it treats other sectors needing support. This issue is underscored by the Kenyan credit system, which is tied to producing title to land.

Second, the state could have favored African firms over multinational firms by insisting on a local quota on all consulting contracts, as is the case in some African countries. This would not only facilitate greater consulting activity on the business side, but would train many locals at no cost to the state in varied disciplines. It is an important issue for AAPAM to look into, for there is evidence that such a ruling in Egypt made a difference not only in terms of numbers but in quality of consultants.

Finally, the state could have recognized that the consulting industry was an important source of national expertise and knowledge and that, in the long term, it should be left to nationals. These views are not unanimously held by all firms, but I believe that they are representative of the firms that have thought about the issues.

Beyond their attempts to get the state to favor them, these small African firms are not organized to systematically have an impact on the sector. They are extremely competitive; many are undercapitalized and must constantly generate work. This is used by bilateral and multilateral donors and government to manipulate them. The problem can be solved by merging to create larger companies, which will improve corporate financial and expertise bases. However, given the extreme diversity of firm focus, the extreme individualism of the founders, and, most significantly, the lack of professional integrity of some firms, this solution does not seem feasible at this time.

Reacting to the criticism that they are expensive and do not generate knowledge (a charge usually made by former colleagues left in the public sector), many of the firms argue convincingly that they *are* in the knowledge business. African consulting firms have the reports to prove that they are generating information that otherwise would not have been generated if left to the extremely overextended universities and research institutes. This is something that AAPAM and similar organizations on the African continent should take seriously.

The other major criticism is that the firms are not genuinely interested in solving clients' problems—that they are only interested in being paid for delivering shoddy work. Behind this criticism is the real fact that local firms are underpaid in comparison to the multinationals. Few of them get paid for their overhead. They scramble from job to job, because the niche they operate in does not generate long-term work. One way to improve the quality of work delivered by these firms is to guarantee them long-term work. This would stabilize their cash flows, allowing them to concentrate on the delivery of quality work.

The criticism of lack of interest in clients is not totally unfounded, however, for it is clear that there are numerous hustler firms. It has been suggested that these could be weeded out by the state, but such an approach would be counterproductive, because many of the bad ones are sponsored by individuals within the state. Since they get work through favors, they are not interested in quality and professionalism.

Perhaps the best way to improve professional standards and interest in clients' work is to organize consulting firms into a professional body that could police the sector. We already have experience with discipline-based professional bodies. It would not be much of a logical jump to organize a body drawing all consulting professionals together.

African consulting firms have had limited access to work in other countries. The firms are young, undercapitalized, and thus not in a position to travel, collect the information necessary, and finally bid for work outside their countries. There is merit in utilizing African firms across borders. First, one is likely to get more relevant advice from a genuine African firm than from the parachuting multinationals. Second, consultants from the continent are more than likely to be cheaper than those from outside. Third, there is an urgent need for the continent to develop knowledge systems that address its unique problems. One way of doing this is to give consultants experience across many countries.

One of AAPAM's issues for the future should be to find ways of improving the information exchange between African consulting firms and potential clients in other countries. This is an idea whose time has come; already an American bank is trying to put together a consortium of African consultants in order to make its operations on the continent less expensive. Since the bank got donor (foundation) money for the activity, there is no reason why an organization of African consulting firms, under AAPAM, could not get assistance to offer services to African countries.

Finally, there is the issue of the traditions that are oppressing us. Too many firms seek to legitimize themselves by aping the large multinationals in their sectors. As a result, they do not venture out to find novel and creative solutions in keeping with the social systems and values of the societies they operate in.

However, having said that, I hasten to add that there are firms that have done extremely creative work, particularly in management of development and project design. True, most have been nudged by unconventional donors, NGOs, and, at times, public bureaucrats who have sought solutions to problems not in the books. For me, this is the saving grace of African consulting. It can grow to develop, adopt, and generate knowledge relevant to our collective situation. Knowledge developed in one African country will be relevant to any other African country because of the interrelationship among them all.

CHAPTER 4

Expatriate versus Indigenous Consultants: An Assessment

IJUKA KABUMBA

This chapter concentrates on the advantages and disadvantages of using international or local consultants or both. Consultants can fall under any of the following categories:

1. *National internal consultant:* A national from inside a given organization in a given country.

2. *National external consultant:* A national from outside the client organization in a given country.

3. *International internal consultant:* A nonnational or foreigner from inside a given organization in a given country.

4. *International/foreign external consultant:* A nonnational from outside a given organization in a given country.

The consultancy organization may be public, semipublic, or private, it may be purely local/national, purely international/foreign, or a joint venture between foreigners and nationals (as individuals or as represented by the state).

This chapter concentrates on categories (2) and (4)—national external consultants[1] and international external consultants. However, much of what applies to category (2) is equally applicable to category (1), just as what is relevant to category (4) will have some relevance for category (3).

The observations herein are based on Africa in general and Uganda in particular. They are a synthesis of the experiences of many individuals and organizations studied or interviewed either in the past or for the express purpose of this chapter. Specific examples are avoided because the aim is not to expose culprits but rather to point out advantages and problems and suggest possible solutions to the latter: to be constructive rather than destructive or polemical. The chapter is divided into three sections. The first deals with international consultants. The second section deals with local consultants. The third and final section makes suggestions for overcoming the disadvantages and resolving the problems so that management consultants, especially the indigenous ones, can be optimally utilized.

International Consultants: Advantages and Problems

The use of international consultants has both advantages and problems. However, in the Ugandan context, it seems to have more problems than advantages. Furthermore, the advantages that do exist benefit not necessarily Uganda but, more often than not, the international consultants themselves when they compete with the local ones. Let us start by looking at the advantages that accrue from the use of foreign consultants.

Advantages

There are five main advantages that international consultants have over their local competitors. First, on the whole, international consultants tend to be better qualified, both academically and in terms of professional specialization. For instance, they tend to have more postgraduate qualifications and are usually more specialized in the more "marketable" fields such as financial management, training, management science techniques, administrative management (for example, organization and methods and office management), and management of development projects.[2]

Second, and connected to the first advantage, is the fact that some international consultants have skills that local consultants genuinely lack. So their use is *potentially* beneficial. I say potentially because, as will be noted later, some international consultants hide information from their local counterparts, which makes the transfer of skills and knowledge difficult.

Third, international consultants tend to have longer and more varied experience than local consultants. There are at least three explanations for such a state of affairs: (1) International consultants are likely to have been exposed to a superior educational system and an education-oriented mass media, especially television; (2) their working environment tends to be more technologically advanced and conducive to the development of expertise; and (3) international consultants enjoy greater mobility (within jobs and within the same country), a factor that would tend to give them a broader experience than their local counterparts are able to acquire under normal circumstances.

Fourth, and partly because of the preceding three factors, international consultants are better and more skillful negotiators. The words of Cornelius Dzakpasu, former Secretary General of the African Association for Public Administration and Management (AAPAM), aptly described the situation pertaining to the use of international consultants: "In the real world of economic development, there is nothing like charity; competition, self and national interests are the predominant factors."[3] The possession of negotiating skills is an advantage that international consultants fully exploit and that enables them to beat indigenous consultants in competition for lucrative assignments, especially where the latter enjoy no "patriotic" protection from the user organization or the government.

The fifth and last advantage is that international consultants are potentially more objective. This is not always true, of course, and it does not mean that international consultants are inherently unbiased. On the contrary, and as human beings, they can be as subjective and biased as anyone else. But because they have no stake in the client organization—except in a few cases in which the organization is a multinational or is being funded externally—they can sometimes afford, or at least try, to be dispassionate and neutral, an opportunity that local consultants seldom have.

Problems

The use of international management consultants is fraught with a wide range of problems, but there are nine crucial ones.

First, international consulting services are very expensive indeed. The remuneration package of an international consultant might go as high as $12,000 a month (in U.S. dollars as of July 1988). In this connection, it is only fair to clarify that this figure has two principal elements: the cost of remuneration proper (that is, basic salary, which, for most international consultants, ranges from $500 to $6,000 a month, plus allowances and personal benefits); and the costs of transport, maintenance, and contributions to such basic items as medical insurance and pension. But it is still true that foreign management consultants are relatively more expensive, given the fact that a local consultant is paid only between $500 and $2,500 a month (in U.S. dollars as of July 1988). This is the case even if the local counterpart is equally or, in some cases, better qualified and doing the same kind and amount of work as the international consultant.

The second problem is closely linked to the first. Because of the great disparity in remuneration and other benefits between international and local consultants, the latter feel that they are being mercilessly exploited. Other citizens who learn of the vast sums (to them) earned by the international consultants become resentful, especially when they realize that the sums are being paid out of a loan that they and their children will have to repay. Such a situation might manifest itself in the form of a subtle withdrawal of cooperation or grudging support—neither of which contributes to the optimal utilization of management consultants.

The use of international consultants regrettably perpetuates the belief that "beggars can't be choosers" and makes recipient organizations and countries feel that they are caught up in a dependency relationship. This third point needs some clarification. Many developing countries, including Uganda, are dependent on international organizations and rich countries for multilateral and bilateral forms of aid. The donors want to ensure that their aid is properly utilized. They have little or no trust in many of the officials of the recipient organizations or countries, some of whom have mismanaged the affairs and funds entrusted to them. The donors end up employing their own people—whom they trust—as consultants, sometimes with little regard for their competence. The aid thus has strings, and because the recipient country is a beggar and truly needy, it is obliged by circumstances to use the consultants imposed on it. It is forced to watch helplessly as some of the aid given with one hand is taken back with another.

Local consultants are thus virtually shut out. The exclusion is real and is sometimes legitimized by rules; for example, one international organization does not permit a person, however well qualified, to be a chief technical adviser for any project in his or her own country. Moreover, even when local consultants are employed as national experts, they are paid in local currency. Although this practice appears to be reasonable, the reality is that it makes local consultancy less attractive than international consultancy.

The fourth problem is that, to a large extent, international consultants are ignorant of the critical and subtle elements in the social, cultural, economic, and political environments in which the consultancy takes place. Yet such elements can sometimes lead to the failure of the assignment or partial or total nonuse of the consultancy output. Unrealistic reports that are put on shelves and permitted to gather dust can be the result of this ignorance.

The fifth problem is that, generally, international consultants appear to be in a hurry to complete their assignments, get paid, and embark on the next assignment. The explanation is that the time given to them by the host organization or country is invariably very little. This may well be the case. However, the fact remains that, as a result, shoddy work is sometimes produced. Sometimes what work is accomplished is not substantial; a good deal of the time may have been spent on such activities as discussing the terms of reference, becoming familiar with the local environment, getting to know the people who matter, and browsing through relevant past reports and related documents. In some cases there is no serious attempt to carry out independent research, and the consultant merely copies what he or she has read in the existing literature on the subject matter of the consultancy assignment. Some international consultants prescribe wholesale solutions drawn from their own home or similar experiences; such solutions are ill-adapted to the circumstances of the host country or organization.

Sixth, some international consultants are difficult to trace after the assignments should further consultation be necessary due to "complications" or the need for follow-up action. There are, of course, extra fees for further consultations, unless the agreement stipulated free service for a specified period following the end of the consultancy. The hiring of international consultants, therefore, may sometimes entail hidden, unanticipated costs.

A seventh problem is that some international consultants hide information from the national counterparts that they are supposed to be training to take over their jobs. International consultants are not necessarily free from the fear of being replaced, so they sometimes try to make themselves indispensable to ensure that their contracts are renewed. National counterparts may be given the cold shoulder; what they say or write might, at best, be belittled or, at worst, plagiarized. As a consequence, local capability is not built up and the country or organization is kept in a state of permanent dependence on international consultants.

An eighth problem is related to accountability. Theoretically, international consultants are supposed to be accountable to the host organization or country. In reality, they tend to want to be accountable to the donors. Indeed, hosts sometimes have real difficulty controlling and supervising foreign consultants who are reluctant to take instructions from "beggars."

Last, international consultants have, in theory, no stake in the user organization or country. This is understandable and should not be emphasized too much in determining their worth. Nevertheless, it potentially diminishes the value of the consultancy services offered and is a fact that competent local consultants can legitimately exploit. The locals have an enduring stake in the organization or country, but for the internationals, the assignment could easily be a pure and simple business deal.

The foregoing constitute the major problems relating to the use of international management consultants. We now turn to local consultants, whose engagement is not necessarily problem free.

Local Consultants: Advantages and Problems

The use of local consultants offers a number of advantages, but it has also its own problems.

Advantages

There are seven main advantages in using the services of local rather than international management consultants. First, local consultants are likely to know the sociocultural, economic, and political environments of the client organization or country. The second advantage accruing from this is the likelihood that a local consultant will produce recommendations that, even if subjective in certain respects, are likely to reflect the profound or inner reality of the client organization.

Third, local consultants generally have a better understanding of the client's problems than their international counterparts. Local consultants have probably lived with the problems for years, and they have easier and faster access to critical information. They know the people to approach for certain kinds of information. Sometimes, they have even been dealing with the relevant dossiers. They are in their own country, among their own people, and are therefore, under normal circumstances, more trusted with critical information than international consultants.

The fourth advantage is that the use of African local consultants is in general cost-effective. Local consultants tend to charge much lower fees than their international counterparts and, in any case, their engagement does not normally involve the use of scarce foreign exchange.

Fifth, local consultants have an enduring stake in the client organization. They want the client to survive rather than perish; after all, they are bound to reap, directly or indirectly, the benefits of that survival. In a way, it pains them to see such organizations being misadvised by external consultants, especially if that bad advice is being paid for out of a loan that they and their children will have to repay. The use of local consultants should, therefore, facilitate accountability.

Another advantage to using local consultants is that such use will lead to the development of skills; that is, using local consultants helps them become more competent not only in their professional disciplines but also in the art and science of providing professional assistance and giving advice. Therefore, the use of local rather than foreign management consultants will enhance the building of indigenous consultancy capacity and capability. The significance of this in developmental terms cannot be overemphasized.

If engaged as consultants, locals, like internationals, will have an opportunity to broaden their experience and enrich their résumés. True, as a result, some of them might eventually leave the country for greener pastures, but most of them are likely to stay. Therefore, the local capability built up should, in the long run, promote self-reliance on the part of African countries.

Last, it is obvious that the use of local consultants leads, or should lead, to institution building. By way of elaboration, it is safe to assert that for better or worse, in most cases it is the local consultants, together with other nationals, who will have to implement the outputs of the consultancy assignments and generally carry out maintenance activities. In order to motivate them and facilitate such implementation, it is better to involve them as consultants even in cases in which foreign consultants are engaged as senior partners. The involvement can be total or partial, but its terms and conditions should be such that no bitterness or frustration is engendered.

Problems

The use of local consultants has its own problems and disadvantages. The economic, political, and sociocultural environments in which local consultants operate are at times unfavorable. They are sometimes not conducive to effective management consultancy, especially from the point of view of the consultant. Circumstances tend not to encourage local consultants to be creative and propose bold and appropriate measures that could solve the problems identified. In some cases, local consultants are not readily acceptable to their own people—the senior officials in government, parastatals, and private enterprises. There is a tendency not to have a high regard for locals' advice even when it contains substance and is backed by solid facts and evidence. There are at least four explanations for this problem. There is, first, the tendency to despise or not take seriously what is familiar or readily available. Familiarity breeds contempt and, indeed, "a prophet is respected everywhere except in his home town and by his own family."[4]

Second, the political and economic interests of the senior officials of the client organization, whether international or local, sometimes come into play. In this case, professional considerations are conveniently ignored. The decision to hire so-and-so—be they local or foreign—is based on a number of ideological, economic, political, and other considerations that, in the end, tend to favor the hiring of international consultants. The motives may range from a desire to give employment to foreign friends to a desire to replenish one's foreign bank account.

Third, the genuine attraction of "made abroad" favors the international and disfavors the local consultant. Observations have shown that when officials in charge of an organization are highly qualified, have integrity, have had sufficient international exposure, are well respected in international circles, and are nationalistic, they are likely to be more inclined to hire or promote the hiring of local consultants. They will also find it much easier to convince the donors that the locals should be given a chance. Officers of the kind just described are usually positively and legitimately self-confident, have no complexes, are relatively satisfied economically, have no fear of losing their job (since they can easily find another), want nothing from the consultant except high-quality advice or assistance, and are keen to promote the interests of the organization and the country. This kind of official or manager is not as easy to come by in the African situation as one might think.

The fourth explanation for local consultants' lack of prestige is that, on the whole, they suffer from what can be described as a mismatch between qualifications on the one hand and experience on the other. They tend to be either very highly qualified academically but woefully lacking in practical experience or very highly experienced but sadly lacking in formal academic qualifications. Because the academically well qualified have limited or no experience and sometimes no published works to list on their résumés, they find it hard to impress client organizations or donors as being sufficiently knowledgeable to be hired as consultants. Highly experienced practitioners with relatively few academic qualifications are unable to command the respect of donors or their representatives, most of whom have both experience and high academic qualifications.

Furthermore, most local consultants lack the marketable qualifications and skills that would make them suitable management consultants. Many tend to have qualifications in fields such as general administration, which are overcrowded and about which much is already known. They lack specialized skills in job evaluation, financial control, and project evaluation. This diminishes their value as consultants and puts them at a disadvantage when competing with their international counterparts.

Another problem is that many local consultants do not seem to appreciate the complications and realities of international politics—some of which have been ably summed up by Michael Bentil.[5] These complications and realities have to be studied, understood, and managed or manipulated by the locals, or else they will tend to lose out to their international competitors.

Because of the foregoing and other factors, locals are sometimes poor negotiators. Either they overprice or, more often than not, underprice their bids. Overpriced bids are, of course, rejected, and underpriced bids lead to overexploitation or noncompletion of assignments because of rising costs and similar factors that should have been built into the agreements. The results are disappointing in both cases. In the first instance, the locals will cry "discrimination." In the second, they will be told: "Don't you see, you can't manage these things." Such statements will normally be made by jealous, unhelpful, or frustrated user organizations or those international consultants who would be only too happy to step in and prove their worth.

Lack of skill in negotiations is a very serious weakness on the part of local consultants. In some cases, when the consultants are acting on behalf of their countries or client organizations, they are made to sign agreements that amount to a sellout. For instance, there have been cases of loan contracts under which as much as 60 percent of the value of the loan is overhead to be paid out to, and enjoyed by, expatriates.

Finally, it has to be admitted that local consultants are potentially less objective than international consultants. This is not because they are inherently biased or incapable of objectivity. On the contrary, many try to control, and succeed in controlling, their passions—both the most violent and the tenderest. Nevertheless, unlike internationals, they are truly part and parcel of the whole thing—directly or indirectly. And many times they are too close to the event or have too big a stake to be neutral. Consequently, there is a tendency for their advice to be less objective. However, this problem need not be serious as long as locals try to be as honest as is humanly possible by distinguishing clearly—in the reports they submit to their clients—between objective facts and purely personal issues likely to be subjective. Furthermore, they should ensure that in their own interest and in the interest of management consultancy, they:

1. Do not disclose or misuse the information obtained in the course of their assignments;

2. Are courageous in the way they tender their advice;

3. Do not get embroiled in the internal politics of client organizations; and

4. Are as objective as the human condition and the demands of discretion permit.

Remedial Action

To conclude this chapter, I would like to make several recommendations. These have a double objective. The first is to ensure that the working relationship between local and international consultants is as harmonious as possible and that any competition between the two groups is healthy. The second objective is to solve the following three problems that are said to hamper the optimal use of management consultancy resources:

1. Failure by governments and other public agencies to put consultancy outputs to efficient use;

2. Negative attitudes on the part of governments toward the use of both local and international consultants; and

3. Limited capability and competency on the part of many management consultants.[6]

In light of the foregoing problems, the following course of action is recommended.

Local consultants should be prepared to compete with international consultants and win or lose on merit. The competition will require plenty of intelligence, hard work, thoroughness, and other qualities—all of which local consultants are endowed with. Local consultants should not be unduly worried about temporary or occasional defeats—when they are beaten by their international competitors—even if some of these appear unjustified or unfair. They should draw comfort from the fact that time is on their side.

However, whenever a local and an international consultant are about equally qualified, the contract should be awarded to the local consultant in order to protect and promote the local management consultancy industry. This should apply whenever the international's lead over the local is five points or less. Nevertheless, the primary stress should be on competence in all its facets rather than on nationality per se. The two, however, are not necessarily mutually exclusive.

Whenever possible, international consultants should go into partnership with local consultants. The partnership can be formal—involving ownership by international consultants of shares in local firms or, in a few cases, the other way around—or less formal and mainly administrative. Furthermore, it need not be initiated by the consultants themselves. The initiator can be the client. For instance, during 1988–89, there was an administrative partnership between an international and several local consultants working on the Uganda Government/World Bank Project on Public Service Performance Improvements in Uganda. The local consultants were not entirely happy with the terms and conditions of their service, but the idea of taking them on was a good one nevertheless. It should be extended to similar projects that, for one reason or another, cannot be entrusted entirely to locals. In this connection, it is good to see that some international bodies are continuing to cooperate with African governments to promote local consultancy expertise. For instance, during 1989–90, the United Nations Development Program (UNDP) funded the work of the Ugandan Public Service Review and Reorganization Commission. Apart from the chairperson, the rest of the commissioners plus members of the secretariat were Ugandans. Such partnerships— legal or merely administrative—are beneficial to all the parties concerned: the consultants (local and foreign), the client, and the donor.

When a local and an international consultant are equally qualified, engaged in the same kind of work, and sharing the tasks on an equal basis, they should be paid the same amount of money, except that the local consultant may be paid in local currency using the official exchange rate. National governments should tolerate, even encourage, situations in which some of their nationals earn substantial sums of money when dividends accruing to the nation are high. As far as possible, African governments should negotiate for technical assistance favoring the use of local consultants.

In awarding contracts, clients should not fuss over local consultants competing as individuals or free-lancers rather than as properly registered consultancy firms. What matters is the individual's capability.

All the same, national associations of management consultants— firms as well as individuals—should be formed to facilitate contact, encourage and promote professionalism and higher standards of performance, draw up and circulate among actual and potential clients a list of their (associations') members, and generally regulate the conduct of members. In this regard, the formation of the Uganda Institute of Management Consultants in June 1988 is a step in the right direction.

At the continental level, the excellent work being done by the African Training and Research Center in Administration for Development (CAFRAD)[7] and the UN Economic Commission for Africa (ECA) should be continued. The ECA and the UNDP, through the Pan African Documentation System (PADIS)—Technical Cooperation Among Developing Countries, African Unit—have already inventoried and published a list of African experts, some of whom are specialists in management.[8] So, although CAFRAD's source is helpful for management consultancy, PADIS's source will help with a variety of fields, including management. What is needed beyond the efforts already made is an umbrella organization similar to AAPAM that can promote management consultancy in Africa. The organization would ensure that partnerships between local and international consultants are acceptable and recognized locally and internationally.

Experienced practitioners with little or insufficient formal education should be humble enough to go back to school—on a full-time or part-time basis—to upgrade their skills, improve on their knowledge, and acquire the qualifications they lack.

For their part, academics with little or no practical experience who aspire to be consultants should go into practice even if this might involve serving under managers who are less qualified than themselves. The idea should be to acquire practical experience. The duration of the stay need not matter: It should vary according to individual needs and can be "massed" or "spread" (involving periods of two or so years, on and off).

As far as possible, practitioners should also be encouraged to do postgraduate training—up to and even beyond the doctorate degree. This means that deliberate efforts should be made to discourage the tendency whereby those who obtain very good first degrees and subsequently acquire postgraduate training are, almost automatically, expected to go into training and research, and those without such qualifications are expected to go into practice. The tendency is dangerous because it presupposes that very good brains are needed only in teaching and research. The truth is that such brains are needed perhaps even more in the world of practice where, especially at higher levels, critical decisions are made that involve a lot of research and affect millions of people. We should allow for greater flexibility in the choice of a career, with brilliant or very well-qualified nationals being welcome in the world of practice.

Generally, the gap between theory and practice should not be exaggerated. There should, at all times, be an effort to integrate research, training, and the world of practice—of management. This integration will greatly contribute to the effectiveness of management consultancy from the points of view of both consultants and clients.

Conclusions

Management consultancy has local and international dimensions that should be identified and managed efficiently in the interest of optimal utilization of the African management consultancy resources. The use by African governments and organizations of international consultants is a good thing. What is bad, and should be avoided, is overreliance on them or their use in assignments that could be competently handled by local consultants. For the next decade or so, there will be assignments that should be trusted entirely to local professionals and assignments that should be carried out jointly by local and international consultants with, as local competence grows, the team leader being a local person. Only in very rare cases, such as when local expertise is unavailable, should there be assignments that are entrusted exclusively to international consultants.

Our unwavering ultimate objective should be that, by the year 2000, the debate over local versus international consultants will have become part of management history. We should, in pursuit of this objective, strive to ensure that African professionals acquire enough expertise to successfully compete against international consultants for consultancy assignments in Africa.

Notes

I am grateful to the following for reading earlier drafts of this chapter: Samwili L. N. Serwanja, Permanent Secretary/Special Duties, Ministry of Public Service and Cabinet Affairs; Michael A. Bentil, Chief Technical Adviser, Uganda Government/World Bank Project on Public Service Performance Improvements in Uganda; and Cyprian Batala, Senior Manpower Planning Economist, Ministry of Planning and Economic Development. I am equally grateful to the participants at the Accra workshop whose comments greatly helped in the revision of this chapter for publication. I nevertheless accept full responsibility for the views expressed here.

1. The United Nations seems to prefer the term *national consultant* to describe this type of consultant—that is, if we are to go by advertisements in which the United Nations Development Program invites applications for "4 posts of national consultants in ILO Project UGA/86/013: Feeder Roads Rehabilitation and Maintenance." See *The New Vision* (Kampala), 4 August 1988, p. 10.

2. For a longer list of fields in which management consultants are needed in Africa, see CAFRAD, *Directory of African Consultants and Experts in Development Administration* (Tangier: Author, 1983), p. i.

3. C. Dzakpasu, "Foreword," in AAPAM, *Public Enterprises Performance and the Privatization Debate: A Review of Options for Africa* (New Delhi: Vikas Publishing House PVT Ltd., 1987), p. vi.

4. Matthew 13:57, in *The Bible Societies—Good News Bible* (New York: Collins and Fontana, 1979), p. 21 (New Testament).

5. M. A. Bentil, "The Impact of International Environment in Public Administration and Management Systems," in AAPAM, *The Ecology of Public Administration and Management in Africa* (New Delhi: Vikas Publishing House PVT Ltd., 1986), pp. 247–266.

6. AAPAM, "Aide-Mémoire on Workshop for Senior Level Policymakers on Optimal Utilization of Management Consultants," held in Accra, Ghana, 22–26 August 1988, p. 2.

7. CAFRAD, *Directory of African Consultants*.

8. See, for instance, UNECA and UNDP, *Directory of African Experts 1984*, vol. 1, suppl. iv (Addis Ababa: PADIS, 1984).

CHAPTER 5

Women and Consulting:
Obstacles and Prospects

HILDA KOKUHIRWA SINKONDE

The purpose of this chapter is to provoke thought on factors affecting women working as consultants in order to establish communication links, to share ideas and experiences, and to explore opportunities for utilizing their capabilities. The number of women going into private business is slowly increasing, and women are joining consulting firms, setting up their own consulting businesses, or working as individual private consultants. Like their male counterparts, female consultants have to compete in the marketplace and face the same problems that men face. In addition, female consultants face a different set of constraints by virtue of being women. Such constraints are basically attitudinal, social, organizational, and psychological. These constraints need to be discussed in the total context of women's participation in employment.

This chapter is based on female consultants' personal experiences and observations and on a limited review of the available literature. The first section of the chapter is a general review of the status of women in the labor force, with a focus on African women's participation in the labor force in rural and urban areas. Most African women are found in rural areas, where they contribute about 60 to 80 percent of the total agricultural labor. The majority of working women in urban areas are found in the informal sector, where skills are not required. In the formal sector of the economy, women are concentrated in the services, such as teaching, nursing, and secretarial work. Women are grossly underrepresented in management. A clear understanding of the general context of women's disadvantaged position in the world of employment is an important first step in the effort to come to grips with issues pertaining to the status, role, and prospects of female consultants in Africa. The second section of the chapter provides an account of experiences that demonstrate the various factors constraining female consultants and suggestions for overcoming these constraints.

Women's Participation in the Labor Force

During the last two decades, women have increasingly been drawn into paid employment. Available International Labor Organization (ILO) world data on employment indicate that about 675 million women are currently at work or seeking employment in the labor market, thus representing more than one third of the total labor force. In 1985, ILO estimates put women at 41 percent of the total labor force in developed countries and 32 percent in developing countries.

Women's economic progress, however, is more complex and precarious than the increasing numbers of women entering the labor market may suggest. In terms of the type of work that women do, and in terms of their status and remuneration, women are still disadvantaged. As Sivard pointed out in her book *Women: A World Survey,*[1] the large influx of women to the labor force has not appreciably changed the nature of work for the vast majority. Nor has it significantly narrowed the gap between men's and women's pay. As Sivard pointed out, there are some important issues arising from the nature of women's work. These issues are discussed below.

Unemployment

A relatively large number of women in paid employment are unemployed or underemployed. Income-earning opportunities have not risen at the same rate as their entry into the labor market. Women's rate of unemployment runs higher than that of men and, according to Sivard, there is more hidden unemployment among women in the form of involuntary part-time work or work in the informal sector. In Third World countries, a large proportion of women are known to be self-employed, often as vendors or doing piecework at home. Women in industrialized countries also represent the vast majority of part-time workers, a fast-growing category of workers since the 1970s. The nature of work in the service industries permits it, and family responsibilities dictate it. The concentration of part-time workers is in the prime age group for employment (age twenty-five to thirty-five), which suggests that many are engaged in this work as a temporary measure—often because of the lack of child-care facilities. Sometimes women work part time because they cannot find full-time employment.

Wage Gap

There is a substantial gap in earnings between men and women, although some differentials have narrowed in recent years due to legislative and other policy measures. Comparisons available for the manufacturing industry (twenty-five countries reporting to the ILO in 1982) indicated that women's hourly earnings averaged less than three quarters of men's. For the few developing countries in the reporting group, the earnings ratio was somewhat lower than in the developed countries.

The ILO attributes the earnings gap mainly to the concentration of women in lower-paying occupations rather than to overt differences in pay scales for the same or similar jobs. However, this does not mean that indirect discrimination that results in lower pay levels does not exist. Indeed, it exists in many forms implicit in recruitment procedures and training and promotion policies that favor men. Although some measures to correct basic pay inequality have been implemented, those remedies that involve structural and attitudinal reforms have made less progress. The minimum-wage laws, for instance, have already been implemented in many countries, both developed and developing. But acceptance of those laws that would provide women broader access to all occupations and higher-paying jobs and the acceptance of equal pay for jobs of comparable worth have been slow.

Job Segregation

Occupational segregation, which is at the root of the inequality of pay between the sexes, has not been affected much by the increased employment of women. Women tend to be highly concentrated in a narrow range of fields and in jobs considered to require less responsibility and skill and are therefore paid less. Relatively few reach supervisory or management positions.

Occupational segregation in the developed countries centers especially in the service sector, which has absorbed the bulk of women's influx to the labor force. For example, in Austria in 1981, 63 percent of women worked in just six occupations out of a total of seventy-five. In Sweden, out of 270 occupational categories, more than 40 percent of women were in just five jobs: secretary, nurse's aide, sales worker, cleaner, and children's nurse.

Usually women's occupational concentration is associated with unfavorable work patterns: lower wages, lower status, longer hours, fewer or no fringe benefits, and less security. Although there have been changes in recent years whereby women have crossed over and entered new fields of work previously dominated by men, women fill comparatively few management positions, and in top management they are extremely rare. Labor market segregation and inequality reflect cultural patterns and stereotypes that are not easily changed. Conceptions of gender-related roles are more extreme and rigid in some societies than in others, but on the whole, both women and men are aware of the differences in responsibilities and status, and both sexes develop self-images from their earliest years.

Change is slow, but it is nevertheless possible. Progress in some areas has begun to show, particularly during the International Women's Decade, which created a lot of awareness about the unequal status of women. In Third World countries, women's organizations and self-help groups have been successful in breaking down the stereotypes and giving women a new sense of self-worth. Legislation and direct support in the form of training and guidance are needed to help women break away from technical illiteracy and narrow career options.

African Women and Employment

Rural Areas

It was observed that despite its generally declining importance in the employment structure, agriculture still plays a central role in the employment situation of African countries, and women contribute about 60 to 80 percent of agricultural production. Wage employment represents only 10 to 15 percent of the total African labor force. Because of the high rate of illiteracy among women, coupled with limited job opportunities in the modern public and private sectors of the economy, the proportion of the female population having wage employment is rather small compared to the total female population in the region. Most women live in rural areas, and their mobility to urban areas, where more wage employment opportunities exist, is limited by the roles and functions they perform.

Although the employment situation of women in rural areas may not seem to have undergone much improvement, governments and non-governmental organizations (NGOs) have made efforts to mobilize women through women's groups spread throughout the rural areas. These groups have obtained support from government and NGOs to start income-generating activities, and the performance of some of these groups has been quite commendable. The main income-generating activities have been handicrafts, poultry raising, textiles, farming, shopkeeping, livestock keeping, grinding mills, restaurants, and local beer brewing. The national women's organizations, religious organizations, foreign governments, and international organizations have contributed quite generously toward women's groups involved in such activities.

The performance of these groups however, has been seriously affected by many problems such as poor management of resources, lack of initial capital, inadequate marketing opportunities, and lack of protection and regulation of products and pricing.

The efforts being made by governments, national machineries for the integration of women in development, and other NGOs to support women's income-generating activities are part of the overall efforts being made by African governments to tackle the employment situation. More effort is needed in designing and implementing comprehensive employment policies for the rural areas. Besides integrated rural development policies, price policies, and the encouragement of popular participation at all levels, African planners should take into particular consideration the role of women in agricultural development and the living and working conditions of women.

Urban Areas

The Formal Sector. Available information regarding women's employment in most African countries indicates that there is no discrimination between men and women as far as employment opportunities are concerned, and that labor laws and policies provide equal pay for equal work and for equal treatment of men and women. However, specific efforts aimed at improving women's access to and status in wage employment have been slow. Overall, women are still concentrated in the low-status and low-paying service sector.

Because of limited educational and training opportunities, coupled with home-oriented curricula traditionally offered to women in educational institutions, their participation in the modern sector as a labor force is also limited. The proportion of African women in the modern sector is about 15 percent. Women who are employed are mostly concentrated in the service sector in teaching, nursing, social work, and clerical jobs. Women are rarely found in managerial and executive positions where planning is done and policies are formulated.

In Kenya, for example, women in the formal sector tend to be concentrated in professional nursing and midwifery, enrolled nursing, teaching, shorthand, and teletyping. There are thirty-two female shorthand typists for every male shorthand typist and twenty-seven female professional nurses for every male professional nurse. Women are also well represented in specialized sales and services, where they account for 37 percent of the total in this sector. In the scientific and technical fields, women are underrepresented. For instance, less than 5 percent of physical scientists, architects, accountants, agronomists, and engineers are women. In government administration and in managerial and supervisory positions, the participation of women is minimal.

Although, in practice, there are no legal or constitutional obstacles to the employment of women or to their entrance into any particular occupational sector, women in Africa are still underrepresented in the scientific and technical fields because of historical and cultural factors that reflect the traditional division of labor and unequal educational opportunities.

The number of women employed in the formal sector in Zambia increased from 24,760 in 1975 to 27,540 in 1977—a growth rate of 11.2 percent. However, about 45 to 48 percent of the total female employees are engaged in community, social, and personal services (excluding domestic service) such as teaching, nursing, and social work.

In summary, women are underrepresented in the formal sector, and those who are employed are concentrated in the "female" occupations. They play a very small role in industry, and their distribution within the sectors is ill-proportioned, since most women are to be found in unskilled, ill-paid jobs.

The Informal Sector. In the informal sector, which continues to play a key role in the urban employment situation, women are better represented partly because jobs in this sector seldom require certification or skills. Entry into all but the most menial jobs in the formal labor market requires the possession of minimum educational qualifications. Given women's low levels of education, the informal labor market, with no educational entry requirements, is their main channel for earning a livelihood in urban areas. The scale of enterprise in the informal sector is small and limited with simple technology. Within this sector, women are usually self-employed as petty retail traders in handicrafts, baked goods, tailoring, brewing, and food vending, or they are hired as cooks, barmaids and housemaids.

The informal sector plays a significant role in providing commodities and services that are either not provided by the formal sector or, when they are, are too expensive for low-income groups. In many cases, government authorities have restricted beer brewing and the sale of food and other items on the streets. Since the informal sector fulfills a need for a large urban population—especially the low-income groups—government and local authorities should pay more attention to the informal sector and assist and facilitate its activities.

Some appreciable efforts have been made in this direction by church and voluntary organizations that have improved on existing activities and created new opportunities, particularly for women and youth. A good example is the Jisaidie Cottage Industries, a department of the National Christian Council of Kenya. The objectives of Jisaidie Cottage Industries are to create employment, market products, and train school dropouts in tailoring, weaving, and handicrafts.

In many countries in West Africa, trading is mainly done by women. They predominate in the markets where they spend most of their time, some with babies and small children. The National Council for Women's Societies of Nigeria has established day-care centers at the marketplaces to enable women with small children to work comfortably without the strain of carrying and looking after babies.

Although generally speaking there has been some increase in the number of women employed in wage labor, they are still largely absorbed in traditional employment sectors. Because many women do not possess the skills that the modern economy requires, more men are employed in the modern private and public sectors than women. Women, therefore, are well represented in the informal sector. A study on women in the urban labor market in Tanzania indicated that they represented about 53 percent of all participants in the informal sector in 1971.

Women in all sectors, in both rural and urban areas, combine work with family responsibilities. Since the number of day-care centers and nurseries is far from adequate in the urban areas, most women have to rely on help from relatives or else hire housemaids. Much housework is still being done using hands and simple outmoded tools and equipment, taking a lot of time and energy. Pounding, grinding, washing, cooking with firewood, and fetching water and fuel are still some of the most burdensome activities in the home. The introduction of appropriate technology could ease women's work loads and increase their productivity. The provision of facilities such as day-care centers, nurseries, training in management, and access to credit necessary to expand women's businesses are a priority.

Female Consultants: Challenges and Constraints

This section discusses women's experiences in consulting, their constraints, and strategies for improving their situation. In the absence of data on women and consulting, and for the sake of discussion, the author held informal interviews with ten female consultants, both African and Western. All these women have worked as consultants for international organizations including the United Nations, the World Bank, the U.S. Agency for International Development (USAID), and various NGOs and government ministries in Africa, Asia, and Latin America. The nature and duration of their assignments differed from one consultant to another, but the fields covered include business management, personnel management, health, family planning, education and training, project evaluation, water and sanitation, nutrition, income generation, agriculture, small business, and food technologies.

The motivations for opting to become consultants were various: being "my own boss," freedom and flexibility, utilizing skills and experience acquired over the years, overcoming stagnation, survival, personal fulfillment, and so on. The one common characteristic among these women is that they all started by working as civil servants.

Consulting as a profession, particularly private consulting, has its own demands. It needs people who have initiative; who are articulate, alert, and aggressive; and who have a strong belief in their own abilities. Private consultants must like variety, be willing to learn new skills, be able to adapt to change, and thrive on uncertainties. They need tenacity, perseverance, and courage to keep going when proposals are rejected and assignments are hard to find. Physical stamina and energy to stand up during long hours of work are essential. Unrealistic deadlines and job pressure require stability and patience. Being on the lookout for assignments, writing out contract agreements, billing for and collecting fees, and legally owning and managing a business all require skills. Any consultant—male or female—needs these strengths in order to be effective and successful. Talents needed to handle roles in private consulting have been enumerated as follows: competitor, strategist, scholar, teacher, listener, communicator, motivator.[2]

Although women, like their male counterparts, may have the talents and skills that make a good consultant, their work is usually constrained by factors that relate to their multiple roles, societal values, attitudes and expectations, and lack of communication links.

Attitudes

The three examples that follow demonstrate the deep-rooted attitudes toward the role of women.

> Example 1. After Janet quit her job as an accountant in a tobacco company where she had worked for eight years, she decided to set up her own consulting firm in accounting and auditing. A job was advertised for which she went for an interview. The interview panel was all male, and at the end of the interview she was told: "Well, Janet, we think that you meet all our requirements, but we are looking for a credible firm that is at least headed by a man!"

> Example 2. Hilda Maps was a member of a two-person team sent by UNESCO to Country X to evaluate an educational project. The team was met at the airport by two officials from the Ministry of Education,

one of whom knew Hilda's colleague Dr. Leo Matata and was excited to see Leo after five years. "Good to see you Leo, and I am so happy and relieved that you have brought your own secretary! Our two secretaries are on maternity leave."

Example 3. Amina is a water engineer, Moses is a public health specialist, and Ray is an expert on women and development. The three-person team was sent to Country A by an international NGO to provide technical assistance in a water and sanitation project that had a women's component. The project manager was thrilled when the team arrived in the country. "This is a perfect team—just what we need, two water engineers and a woman to take care of the women's activities."

The three incidents demonstrate ingrained attitudes about what women are expected to do and what they cannot do. Despite the changing roles of women and their participation in various sectors of social, political, and economic development, perceptions and attitudes toward women's roles have not changed much, if at all. Women have to work several times as hard as men to prove themselves and gain credibility. Discrimination against women is a result of such attitudes.

Family Responsibilities

Consulting, particularly for international organizations, involves traveling away from home for long periods of time. Leaving a family behind can cause anxiety and can strain relationships. The question is, who takes care of the family? In the case of young children, who provides child care? These are questions that male consultants usually do not have to face. Some female consultants with families, particularly those with young children, tend to prefer short-term assignments so that they are not separated from their families for too long. Alternatively, they accept those long-term assignments that allow them to take their families along. Having a supportive family is very important. Family responsibility however, is a factor that affects not only female consultants but all working women. A child-care support system is a critical need for all working mothers.

Communication Links

The following dialogue illustrates the consequences of women's lack of informal support and communication networks.

   Abu: Did you sign the contract?
   Lulu: Yes I did, and I'm very excited about it!
   Abu: So, how much did you charge them for a daily fee?

Lulu: Well, $120 a day.

Abu: That's it—$120 a day?

Lulu: Yes, that's what they offered me, and I think it's a good deal.

Abu: Lulu, do you realize that you sold yourself short? Just consider your skills, experience, and the quality of the work you'll do for them.

Lulu: How much money do you think they should have offered me?

Abu: The key word here is "negotiation." You give them your own rates, time frame, conditions of service, and so on, and then you all sit down and talk, agree, disagree, or keep talking. You have to have your own terms, otherwise they underpay you.

Lulu: I feel very uncomfortable arguing about money, and I usually leave the money question till the end.

Abu: If I were you I would have charged a higher fee. In fact, I would have doubled the fee, because right now the daily rate for that kind of work ranges between $160 and $240.

Lulu: How do you keep track of the going rates?

Abu: A little market research and, of course, the "network." I mean the "old boys' network."

Is Lulu's tendency to undersell herself a result of her underestimating her own capabilities? Is this underestimation a result of Lulu's self-image, which has been shaped and reinforced by the process of socialization? How and when is Lulu going to learn the rules of the game?

Although men belong to the old boys' network, women rarely have an "old girls'" network through which they can support one another and exchange knowledge and information among themselves. Being good at a job is not enough; an individual must also learn to take advantage of informal associations. There is need for all working women, not just consultants, to establish communication links for collaboration in order to support one another; to share views, information, and experiences; and to keep abreast of events.

Prospects for the Future

There are many problems that female consultants face and most of them apply to all working women. The problems that have been listed above are just a few examples. These problems can be overcome if we make an effort. Actions to be taken to solve the problems of African women should not be marginal and separate from those taken to deal with overall development. Many African governments have already acknowledged the importance of giving special attention to women, and strategies to this effect have been adopted at various levels. Actions to implement these strategies must be stepped up.

With regard to female consultants, most of the problems they face are attitude related. These can be overcome through the process of awareness, education, and training. From observation, it seems that the international organizations—particularly the United Nations and some NGOs—have so far taken the lead by employing women as consultants. The number of African women who have gone into the consulting business has increased during the last decade (there are no figures available). To name just a few examples in Kenya, Zambia, Cameroon, Senegal, and Mali: Women have set up consulting firms in small-business training, business management, training in management, development assistance, and other areas. Besides these established firms, the number of female free-lance consultants is also on the rise. Some of these women have offices where they have the advantage of visibility; others are working from their homes.

The challenge now for Pan-African organizations like AAPAM, charged with the responsibility of promoting management consulting, is to identify these consultants and facilitate their visibility so that they can be effectively utilized.

Notes

1. R. L. Sivard, *Women: A World Survey* (Washington, DC: World Priorities, 1985).

2. B. L. Johnson, *Private Consulting: How to Turn Experience into Employment Dollars.* (Englewood Cliffs, NJ: Prentice Hall, 1982).

PART II

Consulting: Organization and Process

CHAPTER 6

Setting Up and Operating a Private Consulting Facility

G. A. HALDANE-LUTTERODT

In a substantial proportion of less developed countries, many of the features of industrialization that characterize a developed economy are hardly visible. During the past two to three decades, many governments, particularly in African countries, have embarked on extensive national development programs. Although they are basically infrastructural, such programs are fundamentally targeted toward industrialization. As a result, many institutional structural adjustments are necessary, demanding the use of both local and foreign technical and management consultants. This situation has led to rapid expansion in the setting up and operation of consulting establishments.

In Ghana, for instance, the Economic Recovery Program (ERP) of 1983, introduced by the government of the Provisional National Defense Council (PNDC), required restructuring of the civil service as well as the public and private sectors of the economy. This stimulated rapid development of private consulting services. Indeed, before ERP, the role and impact of private consulting services had been minimal. This was due in part to the poor performance of the economy and in part to the overreliance of previous governments on foreign consultants. It must be stressed that the emphasis on the development of local consulting facilities in Ghana was largely the outcome of government policy that recognized and addressed the imbalance between foreign and local consulting capabilities.

Organizational Form

The organizational structure of a management consulting firm must be designed to facilitate the provision of services that meet the criteria for professional competence and effectiveness. As a management system, the organizational structure must define areas of functional responsibility and authority, lines of accountability, information flows, and levels of decisionmaking. The dynamics of its operation must also satisfy the requirements of the social, economic, political, and cultural environments. The structure must promote the achievement of corporate objectives, allow growth and expansion, and promote the career prospects of staff. Furthermore, since the organization is expected to represent clients with specialized and sophisticated interests, the consultants must possess the specialized knowledge, skills, and analytic techniques that are prerequisites for enhancing professional competency and organizational viability.

In theory, there are several types of organizational forms. The earlier ones include the centralized functional form, the line-staff form, and the decentralized product division structure. In response to the increasing demands of high technology and the complexity of modern industrial environments, other structures such as the free-form conglomerate and the matrix organization have also evolved.

Along this continuum of organizational forms there are the extremes of product and functional designs as well as different organizational mixes. The design of each is determined by the type of authority structure, integrating mechanism (such as task force, team, group, or committee), desired and formal information and reporting systems. A private consulting firm with either sole proprietorship or multidisciplinary ownership can be structured from among the different organizational alternatives, provided the strengths and weaknesses of each are assessed with respect to the corporate objectives.

The Functional Structure

The most prevalent organizational form in use today is the basic hierarchical structure, with top management at the top of the pyramid, supported by middle and lower managements below. Such an organization is usually broken down into different functional units that define the areas of specialization by management functions: production

management, financial management, accounting and personnel administration, project feasibility preparation, economic and transport planning,
and so on. Indeed, there are many functional areas of specialization on
which a newly set-up private consulting firm with a functional structure
can provide expertise. Specialization by management functions has
become an area of increasing importance, creating a considerable
demand for consulting services because of the ongoing structural
reforms in most developing African countries.

The strength of the functional organization is in its centralization of
similar resources: for example, the engineering or financial department
that provides a secure and comfortable organizational arrangement with
well-defined career paths for junior as well as senior staff.

The functional organization is not without weaknesses:

- When a functional organization has to deal with multiple
  assignments, conflict may arise over the relative priorities
  of different assignments, and there may be competition for
  resources.

- The specialized functional department tends to becomes
  more engrossed in its own specialty than the stated goals of
  the particular project or assignment.

- Problems of administrative inertia together with some
  demotivating factors tend to give oblique perceptions of
  project goals.

The Project Structure

In contrast to the hierarchical functional organization is the single-purpose project or vertical organization. In this type of organization, each
specific assignment or project (and the resources necessary for its accomplishment) is separate from the regular functional structure and is set up
as a self-contained unit headed by a project manager or project consultant. The consultant is given considerable authority over the project and
may seek resources from within or outside the organization. All personnel are under the direct authority of the consultant for the duration of the
project. This structure finds increasing application in sole proprietor-
ships, in which the internal structure is basically functional, with the project team being divided into various functional areas. The project
structure can also be created from within a multidisciplinary organization for a specific assignment or objective.

There are a number of advantages associated with the project
structure:

- The singleness of purpose and unity of command;

- An esprit de corps, developed through clear understanding of and focus on a single objective;

- The effectiveness of informal communication within a closely knit team; and

- The near absolute control over all resources by the consultant.

There are, on the other hand, a number of disadvantages resulting from the imperfections of this structure:

- The setting up of the project organization, possibly from a multidisciplinary consulting establishment, may temporarily upset the normal organization.

- There may be duplication of facilities and inefficient utilization of available scarce resources.

- The job security of team members (depending on initial arrangements) is a sensitive issue, since it is likely that some of the team members will be reabsorbed or laid off when the project is finished.

The project organization, being a single-purpose structure, is output oriented in its design (for example, construction of a new dam or industrial complex). In contrast, the functional hierarchical organization is organized around technical inputs such as financial, marketing, engineering, production, and so on. The problem is that both structures are practically unidimensional in a multidimensional world. It is difficult to get a proper balance between the long-term objective of the functional departments in building technical expertise and the short-term objective of the project.

The Matrix Structure

The matrix organization seems to offer a compromise between the extreme roles and functions performed by the two structures described earlier. Essentially, the matrix organization seeks to maximize the strengths and minimize the weaknesses of both the project and the functional structures. The matrix organization, commonly regarded as a multidimensional structure, combines the standard vertical hierarchical structure with a superimposed lateral structure of a project consultant.

Consequently, the functional department is responsible for *how* the assignment is carried out, and the project consultant specifies *what* has to be done.

The matrix organization not only balances objectives and ensures coordination across functional departmental lines but also permits the project objectives to be observed through the project coordinator's office.

The major disadvantage associated with this organizational form is that the people in the middle are working for two bosses. Vertically, they report to their functional department head, and horizontally or laterally they report to the project coordinator. This situation is likely to provoke organizational conflict if the reporting system is not clearly articulated. Project managers may feel that they have little authority with regard to functional heads, and heads of functional departments may feel that project managers are interfering in their domain. This situation is best resolved by clearly articulating the rules and the responsibility and authority of each of the actors.

Criteria for Selecting an Organizational Form

The criteria for selecting the organizational form of a private consultancy firm must be guided by a number of considerations premised on experience and attention to the total environment.

Experienced and thoughtful managers know that no one particular approach is perfect for all situations. Nevertheless, the current approach being advocated is the *contingency* organizational form. This concept states that the best choice among several alternatives is contingent on the key factors in the environment in which the management system will have to operate. Indeed, the choice of any particular form of organizational structure must be contingent on the level of sophistication and complex nature of economic activities, political and social systems, and cultural values of the society.

These environmental factors are important if the setup is to allow for growth and development in subsequent years. This is true regardless of the ownership structure—individual or sole proprietorship, partnership, unidisciplinary or multidisciplinary.

Organizational Linkages

Any organizational structure must have external linkages, since these are the live channels carrying the information or other elements that facilitate meaningful and rewarding interactions with outside organizations. The universe of institutional or external linkages may include user agencies, sponsors and donors, professional bodies, the general public, political factions, and the chieftancy.

The institutionalization of effective linkages facilitates interactions with financial institutions. It also provides political support and legitimization and helps in obtaining technical assistance from other organizations. Such linkages can also promote organizational interests in government and, particularly, in the industrial environments.

Institutional linkages are separate, identifiable entities that consultants need to interact with regularly. For example, an institutional linkage may be a small group of people or even an individual who has tremendous political clout over matters relating to an important project. Once identified, an institutional linkage has a point of contact in the power structure through which agreements are reached.

In practice, there are a number of institutions with which primary collaboration is essential. These include utilities; industrial, health, statutory, and financial institutions; and clients. When developing institutional linkages, a private consulting firm must clearly distinguish between users, competitors, collaborators, professional bodies, and legal institutions.

In order to be accepted as partner in organizational linkages, a consulting organization must:

- Be readily visible to users or clients as a registered or unregistered entity;

- Be aware of the media for promoting its expertise;

- Comply with professional rules and regulations for securing business;

- Endeavor to acquire professional competence in submitting project proposals;

- Ensure competence in project execution by avoiding delays in completion dates or cost overruns;

- Search for competence in report writing, communication, and development of essential management skills;

- Seek membership in relevant professional bodies in order to become intimately acquainted with norms of private consultancy practices; and

- Be subjected to external pressures requiring the development of an organizational culture, which will encourage spontaneous recognition of the organization.

Management Consulting

Management consulting is a process of providing professional services of an independent, unbiased, and advisory nature. It requires a high degree of professional competence and effectiveness based on sound knowledge, astute skills, and broad analytical capabilities.

Essentially, management consultants are the custodians of all management consulting establishments, regardless of the type of ownership. In the process of providing professional services or demonstrating professional competence and effectiveness, management consultants must possess the ability to plan, organize, direct, and control available human and physical resources in such a way as to ensure the cost-effectiveness of any assignment or project—preliminary surveys, preparation of feasibility studies, detailed project evaluation, procurement inspection, management audit, or more specific assignments such as job evaluation, job inspection, or systems analysis with particular reference to work procedure.

Broadly, management consultants seek to solve what appear to be problem areas to clients. In most cases, the selection of a consulting firm is made through some form of closed competitive bidding. A consultant quotes a fixed price in the proposal to a prospective client and may even be requested to provide a bank guarantee at the time the bid is made. This is to ensure that the consulting firm will be committed to this offer if it is chosen.

Consultancy Costs and Payment Criteria

Before a firm accepts any management consulting assignment, both the consultant and the client should fully understand the specifics of the agreement, including:

- The specific work to be done;

- The standards to be followed;

- The time schedule;

- The methods to be employed for accomplishing the job, monitoring it, evaluating it, and ensuring its adaptive control; and

- The staff assigned: numbers, qualifications, and experience.

The consulting firm ought to be clear about its preferred mode of remuneration. Among the various payment systems within the consultancy profession are:

- Lump-sum payment, used for relatively short-term assignments that are very well defined;

- Per-diem or time-based contract payment, for assignments involving individual experts for supervision, management auditing, and so forth;

- Reimbursement of costs plus a fee calculated as a percentage of costs; and

- Cost plus a fixed fee, which broadly protects the client against profiteering by the consultant, but does not protect the client from having to pay for the consultant's inefficiency. This type of payment is suitable only for consultants known not only for their special experience in the field but also for their integrity.

- Because of continually rising costs, most consultants require escalation clauses in the contracts.

Strategic Planning

The management of a private consulting firm must establish a strategic (or long-range) plan that identifies problems and opportunities in the total environment and outlines long-range objectives and goals, financial plans, policies, and procedures to guarantee the sustained growth of the firm.

For short-term considerations, an operational plan establishes budget objectives, budgets, detailed action plans, and schedules. This then becomes an action-oriented plan for the firm.

With the firm's corporate and operational plans in place, it is the duty of management to organize the resources necessary to accomplish planned goals. Specific activities implicit in the assignment are grouped into a logical pattern and allocated to specific positions or people within the organization.

Once a plan has been formulated and the organization properly structured to accomplish the plan, the third management function—that of directing—stimulates the organization toward its common objectives. Directing is broadly defined as the process of pursuing a certain course of action according to a predetermined plan. It requires leadership and motivation of staff to make sure that their efforts are rationally coordinated and that standards of performance are maintained.

The final step is implementation and control, which establishes reporting systems, ensures analysis and measurement of performance, gives rise to corrective action, and hence brings about changes in objectives and plans.

Within this framework of the management process, management of time (both chargeable and nonchargeable hours) is closely monitored and detailed in the accounting system to ensure effective cost control of the assignment and eventual accountability. This is achieved through the following measures:

1. Job costing, by:

   - Establishing responsibility,

   - Establishing a charge number,

   - Establishing a budget,

   - Establishing a job schedule,

   - Creating the job structure,

   - Making task assignments, and

   - Directing all charges to the job.

2. Standard costing, by

   - Assigning responsibility to line management,

   - Establishing account numbers,

   - Establishing standards,

   - Establishing schedules,

   - Establishing work breakdown by standard items, and

   - Establishing charges gathered by account numbers.

3. An integrated cost-schedule system, which provides a definite basis for measuring cost performance in relation to

work accomplished and ensures that budgeting and scheduling are built on the same data base and are interdependent. This is ensured by requiring that:

- The work is divided into small, discrete, assigned work packages;

- Specific responsibility for the work packages is assigned within the organizational structure;

- The work packages are scheduled, and meaningful completion points (milestones in order to show work accomplishment) are determined;

- Estimates of cost or of the value of each work package are provided;

- The work packages with meaningful milestones are assigned to the lowest formal organizational level; and

- Work accomplishments are recorded by work-package completion, and actual costs consistent with the work-package structure are collected.

All the above activities constitute various aspects of the management process in which the functions of planning, organizing, directing, and control are systematically performed so that the expected results of any consulting assignment are cost-effective.

Thus, for a consulting assignment to be cost-effective, the management of schedules involving cost, time, and work load must be effective and efficient. The consequences of cost overruns, the expected profit margin based on the amount of the contract award, and the likely penalties to be incurred for undue delays in the completion date must all be considered.

It is therefore necessary to ensure that project performance is monitored and evaluated regularly. Efficient reporting or information feedback systems must be in place to engage the attention of management, whether in a sole proprietorship or multidisciplinary firm. In all instances, the main objective of the consulting firm is to make some margin of profit. This is accomplished by means of a management process that ensures accountability and information flows and delineates areas of responsibility and authority and levels of decisionmaking. Therefore, strengthening the structural weaknesses in the management of a private consulting facility should result in improved performance.

The setting up and operating of a private consulting facility must take the fullest advantage of modern management processes to mitigate the complexities and sophistication of the rapidly changing economic, political, social, and cultural environments.

Logistical Support

The logistical requirements of starting a consulting firm include initial financing. This is essential, since lack of funds for initial investment raises the problem of the creditworthiness of the firm. When this problem is circumvented by securing adequate and acceptable collateral in fulfillment of banking requirements, funding becomes available to purchase infrastructural resources such as:

- Transportation for staff in connection with job contacts, visits to project sites, and follow-up on completed or ongoing projects;

- Computers and word processors for information storage and retrieval, preparation of reports and other documents, official correspondence, analysis of complex problems, and so on;

- Facilities for the collation and binding of reports, to make presentations attractive and professional;

- Competent secretarial staff with professional skills and experience in the use of facilities mentioned above;

- A proper filing system that ensures efficiency in the administration and management of the establishment;

- Adequate offices, drawing rooms, and conference rooms; and

- Technical and management reference books, journals, and periodicals.

The urgency to introduce such modern facilities into consulting firms stems from the rapid rate of expansion and the increased sophistication and complexity that both public- and private-sector organizations have recently acquired. Who could have predicted the use of personal computers and word processors throughout Ghana when, only ten years ago, not even electric typewriters were used extensively?

Private consulting firms must offer competitive services if they are to compete successfully with foreign consulting firms. The proliferation of private consulting firms must be seen as a reasonable indication of economic buoyancy and prosperity. Ghana seems to be passing through this phase currently.

The primary considerations in starting a private consulting firm are the type of consultancy services to be provided and the type of collaboration that will facilitate the rapid development and growth of the new establishment. The other important consideration in the initial stages of development is how to promote client interest in the establishment, particularly through brochures. Such a document should include the following:

- A capability statement of the firm;

- An experience statement (i.e., contract assignments accomplished);

- A credibility statement, emphasizing formal or informal professional relationships with banks, professional bodies, and so on; and

- A statement of the firm's capability to do research and search for jobs.

When initial training is needed to acquire further consulting skills, every effort should be made to get it, in spite of the cost. Finally, since cost control of projects is the most important aspect of the managerial function, it must be accorded the closest scrutiny to ensure the viability and profitability of the firm.

CHAPTER 7

Organizing for Improved Consultancy Capacity in Institutions of Higher Learning in Africa

OWODUNNI TERIBA

For the purpose of this chapter, institutions of higher learning (IHLs) include all centers of research and pedagogy beyond the secondary school level. The common feature of these institutions is the existence of both teaching and research, even though the mix of these variables differs from institution to institution. Notable examples of IHLs are the universities and colleges of science and technology and the research, technical, and technological institutes and centers.

From the standpoint of the provision of consultancy services, the pertinent resources possessed by IHLs, again in varying combinations, are (1) the teachers, scholars, researchers, technicians, and technologists; (2) the students; and (3) the research and technical laboratories, workshops, and equipment. All these taken together as a collective pool define a certain potential for consultancy practice. It is one thing, however, for a potential to exist; it is another for it to be properly harnessed or translated into reality. The experience in Africa, so far, is that most of the potential and locked-up talent for consultancy practice in our IHLs have not, for a variety of reasons, been effectively and fully utilized.

In what follows, an attempt is made to examine the general problems of consultancy in African IHLs and the possible approaches to their solutions. The tentative conclusions offered are based largely on the lessons of experience from an ongoing experiment in institutional consultancy at the University of Ibadan, Nigeria. Since some consultancy capacity and activities already exist in many of the IHLs, the principal focus of this chapter is on how to organize for enhanced and improved consultancy capacity: what organizational structures, internal management systems, techniques, and new approaches are required.

General State of Consultancy in African IHLs

There is nothing new about the practice of consultancy in our IHLs. Some of the staff members of these institutions have at one time or another engaged in consulting work. However, consultancy assignments have generally proceeded in a haphazard manner in these institutions, often underground and clandestinely, as an individual rather than institutionalized enterprise.

The uncertain and sometimes hostile reactions of the IHL administration to consultancy are partly to blame for this state of affairs. Some IHL administrators simply turn a blind eye to the consultancy work of staff members, without either opposing or conferring legitimacy on it. Others have taken the extreme position that staff members' earnings from consulting assignments legitimately belong to the IHL that employs them full time and owns the equipment and infrastructural facilities employed in the process. Some IHLs impose arbitrary ceilings on the income staff members can earn from outside employment or assignments, without actually prohibiting such assignments. The reasons for these negative reactions have never been clear. Nor is there necessarily a consensus—either in the community at large or in the immediate environment of the IHL—as to the desirability, objectives, legitimacy and propriety of consultancy practice within institutions of higher learning.

The internal structures and procedures of IHLs tend to differ from those of other organizations normally created for the purpose of making profit. Many people within IHLs take this to mean that it is neither their business nor that of the institutions they work for to engage in consultancy. There are many African governments and public bureaucracies that remain unconvinced of the need for IHLs to participate in consulting or, at best, they are only grudgingly in support. Many people see IHLs' entry into consultancy as a threat to private consulting organizations and firms or as unwholesome, if not unfair, competition that must be resisted at all costs.

The negative reactions to consultancy from within the IHLs have ranged from cynicism and apathy to downright opposition and hostility. The academic purists and fundamentalists, steeped in the orthodox tradition of ivory-towerism, do not want the knowledge industry to be contaminated by the unwholesome pressures of the market, they oppose any official sanction of consultancy practice. Because the opportunities and ability to take part in consultancy are not necessarily evenly distributed among IHL staff members, those who see little or no possibility of consultancy assignments within their own narrow disciplines or horizons would like to selfishly deny others such opportunities.

The point is that there must be a consensus on the issue of consultancy practice in IHLs. Ambivalence on the part of IHL authorities is as unhelpful as outright prohibition. In the case of Nigeria, the government prohibited the private practice of consultancy by individual IHL staff members, but it gave these institutions permission to provide consultancy services as corporate bodies. According to Decree No. 5 promulgated by the federal government, IHL "staff members must not be invited on their own individual basis to render services for which they will receive remuneration. Any agreement that should be signed should be between the client and the university as the owner of the consultancy, and not with any individual members of staff." With this unambiguous statement of support for institutionalized consultancy, the way was clear for Nigerian IHLs to engage in consultancy as corporate bodies. But the government went even further, making the policy decision that all government institutions and parastatals should use the consultancy services offered by the country's institutions of higher learning. These actions by the government created the legal and enabling environment for IHLs consulting practice and guaranteed a certain degree of patronage for their consulting services.

Objectives and Functions of Consultancy in IHLs

Institutions of higher learning exist broadly to cater to the three main functions of teaching, research, and community service. Therefore, the question naturally arises whether there are inherent conflicts between these objectives and the business of consultancy, and whether an IHL's involvement in the latter will jeopardize and adversely affect the former. The broad answer is that there need not be a conflict, depending on what the IHL's consultancy objectives are and how they are managed.

The first point that must be emphasized is that IHLs should not undertake all consultancy services. To do so is to succumb to the "butterfly" approach to, or the "portmanteau" type of, consultancy, which is the bane of many management consulting firms in developing countries. Since successful consultancy cannot be provided without adequate staff, expertise, and necessary backups, each institution must examine its particular circumstances and determine what areas of consultancy work it can effectively undertake without weakening its main functions of teaching, and research.

Given the way that IHLs are generally organized and the part-time nature of any consultancy work they may undertake, the most appropriate types of consulting for these institutions to engage in are advisory services and management consultancy, including socioeconomic studies and project evaluation, feasibility studies and appraisals, and contract research and development work. The flexibility in organizing follow-up tasks in these areas is such that they can easily be accommodated within the work schedules of institutions of higher learning. In addition, no unusually large overheads are involved on a permanent basis. In contrast, engineering and technological consultancy often requires continuous involvement and the maintenance of ongoing overhead facilities, particularly when the project is not confined to mere design work but includes construction and project supervision. Institutions of higher learning are probably neither willing nor able to be involved in the day-to-day supervisory tasks involved in engineering projects, which may be located far from the campus. Since there is no guarantee that any particular institution will have enough such jobs at any given time to justify the required overheads, the choices are not to contract for such jobs at all or to be willing, if possible, to subcontract the supervisory aspects involved. (But should not design and supervision be intertwined in most engineering consultancy jobs?) The best solution may be for IHLs not to consult as principals on technical projects, but to serve as consultants to the full-time consultancy firms and organizations in those areas. This could open up a mutually beneficial area of cooperation between private- and public-sector consultancy.

The decisions on the appropriateness of particular types of consultancy should be guided not only by considerations of technical capability and availability of expertise and skills in the IHL, but also by the broad objectives and aims of consultancy in such institutions. Such a list of objectives would obviously vary among institutions as heterogeneous as IHLs, but the following list represents the general objectives of consultancy in IHLs:

- To provide opportunities to fully use the existing on-campus intellectual potential and human resources facilities to the mutual advantage of the individuals concerned, the institutions themselves, and the community at large;

- To generate more funds for the institution, with a view toward improving its financial situation;

- To promote cross-fertilization of ideas and activities by bringing town and gown together more concretely and with symbiotic results; and

- To increase the practical and research opportunities and experiences available to students, academics, and other professionals in these institutions to enhance their professional training and practice.

As long as consultancy in IHLs is organized on an institutional rather than an individual basis, there seem to be no inherent conflicts in the pursuit of the above objectives and of those that are regarded as the basic objectives of IHLs. The emphasis, for most, would be on the performance of public-oriented services through the efficient use of the expertise and talent already available within the institutions. Above all, the institutions, as corporate bodies, stand to gain financially by sharing in the proceeds from consultancy jobs. Through consultancy practice and service, IHLs can stimulate innovation and the process of technological transfer. They can help companies and individual entrepreneurs develop new ideas and assess project potentials. In all this, they need not necessarily operate in competition with private-sector consultants. On the contrary, they could be complementary—with consultancy units in IHLs using expertise and talents both from within and outside their campuses and organizations to help industry and government, as an adjunct to and in support of private-sector consultancy efforts.

There are, of course, many allegations to the contrary, coming especially from the people who least understand what consultancy is all about and what its modus operandi is. One such allegation is that IHL staff's involvement in consultancy can be pursued only at the expense of effective and quality teaching. The accusation is that those who engage in consultancy would not carry their maximum work loads or that they would teach rather perfunctorily.

Another allegation is that the pursuit of consultancy necessarily discourages research and hampers publication output and productive scholarship—that teachers who engage in consultancy do not have enough time to pursue basic research and write academic papers and books. Another implicit accusation is that there is so much money to be made from consulting that IHL staff members are likely to be corrupted by the "evil" and unsavory influence of that money and be diverted away from the pursuit of academic excellence.

Experience at the University of Ibadan hardly bears out any of the above allegations, although this does not mean that it has been immune to such accusations. The evidence so far, since the inception of organized and institutionalized consultancy at the university, is that the staff members who have excelled as consultants in the university's Consultancy Services Unit are almost invariably the same staff who have excelled in research, publication, and teaching. Most of the leading consultants have continued to earn their promotions promptly. They are respected leaders of thought in their respective fields and areas of specialization.

This positive relationship between consulting activity and academic excellence probably derives from the fact that consulting often has academic components, or it may in itself be an adjunct of some academic program. If effectively exploited, many consulting activities can in fact enrich teaching, research, and publication while they are, in turn, facilitated by the latter. Take teaching, for example. The fact that a teacher participates in consultancy may make all the difference between remaining a theoretical text-book teacher or becoming a practical real-life teacher as well. Consultancy has on many occasions provided the much-needed bridge between ivory-towerism and societal relevance. But above all, it is a learning process for all concerned: The clients who are paying for consulting services do not do so simply for charity; they want to get something out of it. The teachers and researchers who give some of their time to consulting may do so for the extra reward and income, but in the process, they acquire a tremendous wealth of experience from which they and their students, the IHL, and all of society can benefit.

Structure and Organization of IHL Consultancy

Whatever the origin of the initiatives or the pressures for formally instituting consultancy in IHLs, there is a need for well-defined organizational structures. Rules and regulations to guide the conduct of consultancy must be made and monitored to ensure that both the primary objectives of the IHL and the satisfaction and protection of the clients' interests are not jeopardized or compromised.

Right from the inception, an apex unit, board, or center must be established, under whose aegis and umbrella the consultancy work will be carried on, guided, and supervised as a business venture. The various operational departments, subunits, and centers of consultancy in the IHL will operate under this unit. The alternative is to allow the field of consultancy to remain the unregulated jungle it has been in many IHLs. The functions of the consultancy board, unit, or center include the following:

- To identify and approve areas of consultancy that could be profitably explored;

- To determine the overall policy for disbursing proceeds from consultancy assignments, bearing in mind the interests of the IHL and the need to motivate high standards;

- To determine the remuneration and conditions of service of key management personnel of the center, unit, or board; and

- To receive and consider annual reports from the general manager or managing director of the board, center, or unit.

Each IHL has a choice between incorporating such a unit as a company, in which case the unit and the IHL that owns it would be legally separate entities, or organizing it as one of the many administrative divisions within the IHL. Incorporation and nonincorporation have their respective advantages and disadvantages. Regardless of the mode chosen for institutionalizing consultancy in the IHL, the relationship between the IHL and the consultancy unit must be almost total and must be carefully managed for optimal results. For one thing, the bulk of the consulting jobs will be done part time, by IHL staff who are already located and distributed by disciplines in the various faculties, departments, and research laboratories, using time, equipment, and facilities already procured or paid for by the IHL primarily for academic work. For another, the IHL will have to find the initial capital outlay or seed money to start the consultancy venture. Thus, effecting a profitable functional relationship between the IHL and the consultancy unit is fundamental; otherwise, the exercise may become largely counterproductive.

The structure of the consultancy unit must be dictated largely by the functions that have been mapped out for it. What is most certain is that the structure will have to be more business oriented than the existing cost centers and administrative structures within the IHL.

The consultancy unit needs a board of directors or a governing council of its own, whose membership must be carefully composed to reflect and accommodate all the varied interests in the IHL involved with consultancy and its results. The board's responsibility is to undertake general policy formulation and see to it that the affairs of the consultancy unit are effectively and efficiently conducted, in line with those policies. However, the unit itself, not its board, must be seen as the apex organization for consultancy work in the IHL, under whose umbrella and general management exist the various subunits and operational arms.

Among the operational functions relating to the practice of consultancy (or indeed, of any other business)—general management, production, marketing, finance, accounting, personnel, administration—there are those that are best performed centrally, by the apex unit; those that are best performed at the departmental or subunit level; and those that can be performed at both levels. There are no hard-and-fast rules about the division of labor, but decisions must be made early. It is best that the accounting and finance functions be centrally performed, but the production and marketing functions could be performed concurrently at both levels.

Whatever the final arrangements are, it is necessary to procure, right from the beginning, the services of a full-time general manager or managing director of the central consultancy unit and to provide that person with a package of incentives as opposed to the normal salaries and conditions of service for IHL faculty and department heads. In the University of Ibadan Consultancy Services Unit, the general manager was treated as a consultant whose remuneration consisted of a salary plus a profit-related bonus. In addition, an accounting officer must be recruited and charged with the responsibilities of evolving the necessary financial accounting for the unit independent of the operational procedures of the general accounting system in the IHL.

In fashioning the organizational structure of the consultancy unit, there are a number of alternatives and choices. On the one hand, a fixed number of departments, say three or four, could be established directly under the central or apex unit, with each department headed by a full-time or part-time director or manager. On the other hand, it is possible to have a model whereby the existing academic faculties are regarded as or constituted into departments or cells in the functional areas of production, with each department or cell headed by a manager or director. These two alternatives can also be combined to form a third option. In deciding on the best alternative, it is important to bear in mind the need for economy and, given the cyclical fluctuations in the fortunes of consultancy, to keep overhead costs to a minimum.

The relationship between the central consultancy unit and the part-time consultants through whom consultancy assignments will be carried out on a brokerage basis needs to be clarified. It has to be made clear that no consultant within the IHL can undertake a consultancy assignment that has not received the approval of the managing director or general manager of the central consultancy unit. It should also be abundantly clear that this same official has sole responsibility for the management and control of funds, all contractual agreements, and the monitoring of timely and efficient execution of consultancy assignments within the IHL.

Nonetheless, the activities of the central consultancy unit must per force be subject to the overall control of the governing council of the IHL, to ensure full accountability and consistency with the overall goals and functions of the institution. This can usually be achieved by having the executive head of the IHL or her or his nominee serve as chairperson of the consultancy services board of directors. Through this person, periodic reports on the activities of the consultancy unit will go to the governing council of the IHL for evaluation and scrutiny.

In the case of the University of Ibadan, the Consultancy Services Unit has primary responsibility for the overall management and coordination of the consultancy practice. The managing director, who is a full-time employee of the unit, is the chief executive, but he is supervised by a board of directors, whose chairperson and members are appointed by the vice chancellor of the university and serve on a part-time basis.

Under this umbrella organization are the faculty-based consultancy committees, each headed by the faculty coordinator as chairperson. The faculty committees are supposed to manage and oversee the consultancy activities at the faculty level within the general guidelines and under the supervision of the university's Consultancy Services Unit. The main functions of the faculty coordinator, as the chairperson of the faculty committee, are to serve on the board of directors of the Consultancy Services Unit and to coordinate and develop consultancy activities at the faculty level.

The only full-time staff are the managing director and the finance and accounting officer of the Consultancy Services Unit and their support staff. All other personnel involved with consultancy administration or project execution at the university are part time. All the participants in the actual business of consultancy—the subunits, the individual staff members, and so on—are presumed to be agents of the central consultancy unit. Only the managing director of this unit acts as principal when it comes to signing consultancy contracts between clients and the university, and he is responsible for the overall conduct of consultancy business in the university. The Consultancy Services Unit reports annually to the University Council through the chairperson of its board of directors. The faculty committees report annually to their various faculty boards on the overall results and progress of consultancy within individual faculties.

Disbursement of Consultancy Proceeds

For IHLs to benefit financially from the practice of consultancy by staff members, there must be provisions and built-in mechanisms for ensuring the IHL's access to a given percentage of the contract value or cost of consultancy assignments. The percentage deductions, which must be paid directly into the coffers of the IHL, cannot vary except at the discretion of the board of directors of the central consultancy unit. Such deductions represent, in effect, a charge for overheads. Additionally, the central consultancy unit should have access to another given percentage of the contract value or cost of consultancy assignments purely for its own administrative and operational expenses. Taken together, the two transfers—one to the IHL and the other to the central consultancy unit—represent the minimum that will have to accrue from any project, irrespective of whether a net profit is made. When a net profit is made after all legitimate items of cost have been accommodated, including the consulting costs of the consultants, some formula must be devised for profit sharing among the principal parties involved: the IHL; the central consulting unit, the academic departments and faculties involved, and the individual consultants to the project.

It is important that staff members who participate in consultancy by writing proposals, procuring jobs, executing projects, or through a combination of any of these tasks are fairly remunerated. The IHL must also derive benefits as a corporate body. A judicious balance needs to be maintained in terms of the remuneration of consultants, on the one hand, and the benefits accruing to the IHL and its organs, on the other. The benefits need not be measured in only financial terms, however. The consultancy practice may lead to the buildup of and improvements in the physical infrastructural research facilities as well as enhanced academic performance. These factors must be recognized and taken into account by all concerned in the rewards and benefits equations.

In addition, there is the issue of interpersonal equity in the disbursement of consultancy funds. It is important that individual consultants are remunerated in relation to their contributions, efforts and productivity. Acceptable guidelines must be drawn up, judiciously implemented, and monitored. There is no unique formula, but whatever formula adopted must be fair and equitable.

Using essentially the disbursement approach described above, the practice at the University of Ibadan is to reserve between 15 and 25 percent of the contract value of each consultancy assignment for the university as a whole, out of which 5 percent goes to the faculty and/or the departmental consultancy unit, and another 5 percent is given to the central Consultancy Services Unit.

Conclusions and Recommendations

There are many issues and problems involved in the management of consultancy services in IHL. First is the prevalence of negative attitudes toward consultancy practice in IHLs. Therefore, it is essential to focus not just on the business and economics of consultancy, but on the sociology and politics of consultancy as well if consultancy in IHLs is to take firm root and be built on a solid foundation. There must be a clear and unequivocal statement of endorsement of consultancy on the part of the authorities concerned. If an IHL is going to engage in consultancy, the necessary legal and enabling environments must be created, and this has to start with the responsible authorities—governments and the governing councils of the IHLs—making the necessary policy statements of endorsement. It is clear that without a positive and encouraging attitude on the part of the administration of IHLs, consultancy is unlikely to thrive in these institutions.

Second, the objectives of consultancy in IHLs must be clearly and unambiguously spelled out. Consultancy cannot be allowed to impair the basic functions of teaching and research; it must be seen primarily as an extension of the third basic function of IHLs—community service—serving as a laboratory for the problems of the larger society as well as a nursery bed for some of the preferred solutions. The IHLs must make it clear that consultancy practice is not a matter of life and death, and that only consultancy assignments that fit into their particular areas of competence and capability will be undertaken. In short, it is essential that IHLs, in their bid to capitalize on consultancy practice, do not lose sight of their cherished traditions, ideals, and ethics. Rather than engage in an all-out competition with private consultants in all areas of consultancy, IHLs may be wise to pursue what I call innovative consulting, whereby IHL consultants make themselves available to private-sector consultants in certain knotty areas of consultancy practice. The focus of consulting in IHLs should be on gap-filling and leadership, especially in the grey areas of management and developmental consultancy. This requires IHLs to redefine their mission and to transform themselves into new institutions that are more responsive to the times, more forward-looking, and more imaginative and effective.

The demands of the business and economics of consultancy are such that consultancy practice in IHLs is better carried out openly in organized and institutional form than surreptitiously by individual staff members. It is only within the context of institutionalized consultancy practice that all the parties concerned can be guaranteed an equitable return. This means that appropriate structures for the conduct of organized consultancy must be evolved by the IHL, a key element of which is the setting up of a special unit to coordinate and plan all consultancies in the institution. To avoid the pitfalls of unplanned, ill-organized and disjointed consultancy, IHLs need a well-structured institution-wide framework that—although semi-independent and enjoying some measure of controlled freedom—must, in the final analysis, be subject to the ultimate direction of the governing council of the IHL. The performance of a given consultancy unit, particularly in the early stages, will depend to a large extent on the drive, enthusiasm, vision, and diligence of the managing director. It is essential to recruit the right person and to provide her or him with the necessary challenges and a package of remuneration and incentives that is commensurate with the task.

Besides general guidelines related to the do's and don'ts of consultancy, rules and regulations designed to provide a code of conduct for the practice of consultancy and to address the sharing of consultancy proceeds and profit must be devised. Here, the important thing is to evolve a general formula that is both rewarding and equitable to all parties concerned: the IHL in terms of a good return on its investment, and guaranteed funds to cover its overhead; the consultancy unit in terms of funds to cover management and administrative expenses; and the individual staff members in terms of financial remuneration and rewards commensurate with consultancy expertise and efforts. How large the overall benefits accruing from consultancy practice in IHLs will be depends largely on how well managed the consultancy practice is.

The implicit assumption in all the above is that there is a ready-made and pressing demand for the consulting services of IHLs, and that the real problem is only on the supply side—hence the focus on how to strengthen the capacity for consultancy in these institutions. I venture to suggest that this is not necessarily the case, given the lack of credibility and the inherent suspicion, maybe even distrust, of academics within the wider society as theoreticians. In short, the demand for the consultancy services of some of our institutions of higher learning may have to be created and cultivated. This means that, in addition to organizing for improved consulting capacity and increased public confidence in the practical ability to deliver on time, IHLs must promote their services to the public. Their strategy must never be to wait to be invited. Rather, just as good businesspeople advertise their wares, the strategy of an institution of higher learning must be to aggressively advertise its services and procure jobs by submitting unsolicited but imaginative proposals and cost estimates to clients. Such proposals may center purely on research and advisory activities, or they may relate to the organization of training workshops, seminars, or a combination of both.

CHAPTER 8

Setting Terms of Reference: Issues and Roles of Consultants and Clients

JAMES NTI

There is a growing concern about the fact that available consultancy resources in Africa are not being properly and optimally used. In this connection, the drawing up of the appropriate terms of reference—which could be said to be the starting point of a consultancy assignment—has an important contribution to make to the optimal utilization of consultants.

The use of the phrase "terms of reference" is not restricted to consultancy assignments. It could be used in relation to tendering or contracts, but since the theme of the book is optimal utilization of consultants, the use of the phrase throughout this chapter is restricted to consultancy assignments only.

Terms of reference establish what should be done during the assignment. They serve as a brief to the consultant and provide the framework for a consultancy assignment. They not only establish a program and a point of reference for the consultant, but also enable clients to monitor the consultant's work and satisfy themselves that the assignment has been performed as envisaged.

When Does One Set Terms of Reference?

The need to draw up consultancy terms of reference arises when an organization's top management, faced with certain difficulties, decides that an unbiased opinion from an outsider would be welcome or that advice or assistance is needed in solving certain problems. In other words, the necessity for setting terms of reference arises when top management has decided that there is a need to turn to consultants for help.

Top management turns to consultants for a number of reasons. For instance, management may feel that the organization is not performing or functioning as well as it could or should, but it may not be clear about what precisely is wrong or what the causes are or how to remove the constraints to ensure better performance. In the private and industrial sectors, where results can be quantified, it may be easier to detect the overall malfunctioning of an organization. It could be that there is loss of profits or that sales are declining, which would indicate apparent loss of the organization's market share. In service organizations, where it is more difficult to assess performance, indicators such as mounting public complaints, delays in processing requests, and lack of discipline must suffice. In some cases, there may be no immediate problems; management, having heard of new developments or techniques in the management field, might want a review of the methods or systems in use in the organization in order to keep up-to-date. Management may also want a consultant's advice about the need for expansion or diversification.

There are many other issues for which a consultancy may be needed: feasibility studies for new investments, planning or designing new projects, market surveys, collection and analysis of data to help with long-term planning, investigation of serious misdemeanors committed by staff, and so on. In this context, consultancy may be sought when the organization either cannot afford the staff time or does not have competent staff with the necessary specialized knowledge.

Who Draws Up Terms of Reference?

It is up to the one who needs help to make the first move. When an individual is ill, he or she approaches a doctor and describes the symptoms. When an organization wants a donor agency to finance a project, it prepares a project document indicating what the project is about, what the objectives are, what contribution the project can make to the overall welfare of the organization, and the extent of assistance needed. In the same way, terms of reference are meant to pinpoint the help required from the consultant. Consequently, terms of reference should normally be drawn up by the management or client that needs a consultant's help or advice.

However, owing to a lack of training—or indeed a lack of training opportunities—in this area in African countries, each manager has his or her own concept of how terms of reference should be written. As a result, all sorts of flawed terms of reference may be drawn up.

In some cases, when top management has made a real effort to identify the problems a consultancy should address, the terms of reference are really a string of requests—the consultant should do this, that, and the other. Instead of concentrating on the major, broad themes to be covered by the consultancy, management spells out in detail the activities that need to be undertaken by the consultant, as if it were preparing a project document. Quoted below is an example of such terms of reference.

1. To examine the present structure of the Education Department in relation to the Ministry of Education. This will involve careful consideration of the present system of Regional Education Centers situated in each of the regions, which are extensions of the Department of Education.

2. To make recommendations on ways and means of integrating the functions of the existing Department of Education into the Ministry of Education to create a single administrative/ management unit. Within these recommendations should be indicators of where cost savings can be made and of the structure and post functions of the newly established Ministry.

The first term of reference could have ended after the first sentence. It is not necessary or proper for the client to tell the consultant how to conduct the consultancy assignment. The second term of reference prejudges the issue and gives an indication that the first term of reference, which gives an impression of objectivity, is fallacious.

In some cases, terms of reference for, say, a consultancy on administrative reform have included as many as twenty separate items. This "questionnaire" approach may achieve specificity and ensure that the consultant addresses all the problems the client has in mind, but it does not allow for any flexibility for either the consultant or the client. Some consultants would stick very closely to the questionnaire, find specific answers to the questions posed as quickly as possible, and avoid getting into other related matters that may have provided useful insight into the problem at hand. In such a situation, the objectives for which the consultancy was requested may not be achieved or may be only partly achieved. In other words, there are times when open-endedness in the terms of reference enables the consultant to cover a much wider field and thereby achieve a more comprehensive coverage of the issue being studied. This can be achieved without losing direction by concentrating on major, broad themes.

Listing a series of activities might also result in obfuscation of the major issues that need to be addressed, resulting in an inability to see the forest for the trees. Furthermore, since as many ideas as possible tend to be thrown in, the activities listed may not be in a logical order. This problem is clearly illustrated by the terms of reference for a consultancy on administrative reform. The list of activities that served as terms of reference could have been grouped under four major themes (see the Appendix for the complete, original terms of reference) Numbers (1), (2), and (6) were about the levels of government employment and whether all existing posts were essential to provide the current level of services—a staffing problem. Items (4), (10), (11), and (16) had a bearing on staff development; items (5), (12), (13), (14), and (15) concerned pay, grading, and efficiency; items (3), (7), (8), (9), (17), (18), and (19) raised issues related to restructuring the organization and performance improvement.

The consultant for the assignment, after discussion with the users, condensed the lengthy terms of reference into four basic broad issues that required examination and consultancy advice.

This example may have been the result of the pressure of work and management's lack of time to think through the problems and their relationships. Such a situation can create a lot of problems if the consultant does not have the foresight to group the list of activities into major themes. For instance, it could result in a team of consultants with different expertise criss-crossing paths and subjecting staff members to interviews on the same subject by different experts at different times, leaving them little time for their work and creating frustration and antagonism against consultants. The consultancy report resulting from such a situation is bound to be disjointed and illogical, though it would have been prepared strictly according to the given terms of reference. Certainly the objectives may be the first casualty of such an endeavor.

There have been cases in which top management has made a genuine attempt to concentrate on the major issues but has failed to write clear, objective terms of reference. A case in point is a top management that was requesting a staff audit of its organization. The draft of its terms of reference began with, "A staff audit to substantially reduce or eliminate unemployed, medically unfit, aged, or otherwise unnecessary staff." Even though the document was entitled "Draft Terms of Reference for a Local Government Staff Audit," the terms of reference included matters related to staffing, staffing levels, quality and training of staff, terms and conditions of service of local authority staff, the role of a local government staff commission, and the relationships between the central government and local authorities. In other words, though the title of the assignment envisaged a particular focus, the terms of reference diffused the focus.

In other cases, top management may see only the symptoms and mistake those as the disease or the real cause of the difficulties. Being deeply involved in a situation, management may become subject to "tunnel vision" and may not realize the magnitude or depth of the problem. Terms of reference drawn up under these circumstances might serve to divert an inexperienced consultant from addressing the real issues.

There are times when, in an effort to hide its own blunders, top management may deliberately pretend not to know the cause of the problem and may deliberately indicate causes that lead the consultant on a wild goose chase. It must be pointed out, in all fairness, that some managers have genuine uncertainties, mainly due to their background and training.

Some of these problems in defining terms of reference have resulted in managers' tendency to think that it is the consultant's responsibility to "discover" the real problem, and thereby earn her or his fees. The attitude of some clients is: "If I knew the real problem, I might be able to find a solution to it and there would then be no need for a consultant. By recognizing that I have problems and need help, I have done my duty."

This argument is flawed. For example, it would be ridiculous for a sick person to go to a doctor and just say, "I am sick," and expect the doctor to diagnose the disease without further assistance from the patient. In normal circumstances, patients tell the doctor as clearly and precisely as possible what is wrong, even though they may not know the actual disease that is plaguing them.

It is thus the responsibility of clients who need the help of a consultant to define the problem, as they see it, as precisely as possible, so that the assignment can be properly done. As Kubr puts it, "The client is mainly responsible for defining the objectives of the consultation."[1]

However, consultants worth their salt should, before accepting a consulting assignment, ensure that they can subscribe to the client's definition of the problem. How a problem is defined indicates the approach and method for solving it and limits the options available for its solution. It is important for consultants to check the problem definition, since the problem may be more or less serious than a client thinks. Some consultants prefer to carry out a quick preliminary survey of the organization before accepting any terms of reference. Clients may have committed the common error of mistaking symptoms for problems; they may have been influenced by preconceived ideas or their own educational and training background. Therefore, as often happens, a consultant's definition of a problem may differ from a client's.

How to Help Clients Define Better Terms of Reference

The drawing up of proper terms of reference is the joint responsibility of the client and the consultant. The consultant, therefore, has to take a number of roles: educator and trainer, helping the client identify the real problem areas; problem solver, helping to maintain objectivity and stimulate ideas and interpretations when formulating and clarifying problems; fact finder, providing information for the proper diagnosis of the problem; and process counselor, jointly diagnosing the problem with the intent of transferring to the client the skills necessary to undertake such diagnosis in the future.

It is in the interest of the two parties in a strong spirit of collaboration, imbued by a shared desire for a successful outcome, to compare definitions of the problem and, through discussion, agree on a joint definition. In open-ended management problems, the client rarely hits on a satisfactory problem definition at the outset. And the more one studies a problem situation, the more likely it is that an earlier definition will need to be revised. This happens in consultancy assignments. Managers who engage consultants should, therefore, be open-minded and flexible enough to change the terms of reference of a consultancy based on new information.

Many organizations are now using management or diagnostic surveys to identify the problem and draw up proper terms of reference for the consultancy assignment. In some cases, a management survey is the first step in a consulting assignment; if it is properly done, it helps identify the problem for which a consultant's help is needed.

> The purpose of the management survey is to review the resources of the client, examine the activities they generate, assess performance and identify opportunities for improving the results achieved. The client organization's expansion potential is rapidly assessed, its strengths recognized, weaknesses that need to be remedied uncovered and underlying problems defined.[2]

Such a survey should result in the preparation of a specific proposal on the objectives of the assignment, that is, the specific terms of reference for a consultancy assignment.

A management survey is particularly necessary when a problem is unclear or the client has some uncertainties. In such a case, discussions with the survey consultant may clarify the client's thoughts about the problem, reveal problems that a consultant can assist in solving, or reveal both problems and opportunities that may have been overlooked.

Management surveys, however, have a serious disadvantage: The organization usually gets hooked on the consultant or consultancy firm that did the diagnostic survey and drew up the terms and reference. Management tends to feel a moral obligation to give the survey consultant the consultancy assignment, even though another consultant may be better qualified to bring the ailing organization back to good health.

Management problems for which consultants are normally called in can be categorized into three types: corrective problems (the need to rectify a deteriorating situation), progressive problems (the need to improve an existing situation), and creative problems (the need to create a totally new situation).[3] Clients must make every effort to ensure that there is definitional clarity. Instead of just describing the overall situation or drawing up a shopping list, the key issues must be isolated. To achieve this, one needs to be in a relaxed state of mind, in an atmosphere that is conducive to concentration on the problem under consideration. In this connection, Tudor Rickards suggests an interestingly simple device to set up new thinking patterns, namely, trying to complete a sentence such as: "What I would like to do is . . ." or "If I could break all the constraints I would. . . ."[4]

In defining a problem one makes a statement about its boundaries, but one should be able to accept that these boundaries are open to modification. The point is that a problem definition should not be treated as immutable. If the problem statement is examined phrase by phrase, most of the hidden assumptions will surface and it will become clear that its boundaries are flexible. Another method of redefining a problem is to turn it on its head and examine the paradox.

The Need for Training

The foregoing indicates that some form of skill in drawing up terms of reference is necessary and that clients must avoid an amateurish approach to that exercise. In other words, there is a need to train clients how to take maximum advantage of the consultants they engage. Such training should help them acquire the skills to draw up terms of reference that ensure that the real problems plaguing the organization will be addressed by the consultant. It should help clients clarify what the consultancy assignment should achieve and how such results will be measured.

Since most indigenous consultants in Africa have not had any training in consultancy, they may also need training in properly diagnosing the ills of organizations, identifying the real nature of the problems they are called in to solve, and acquiring the professional method of drawing up terms of reference.

The need for such training is urgent, and African institutions for management training should follow the example of the Administrative Staff College of Nigeria (ASCON) and establish training programs in consultancy for both indigenous consultants and clients.

In the present economic situation of most African countries, such training cannot wait. The more precisely and professionally the terms of reference are drawn up, the better the consultancy assignments will be carried out, and the more cost-effective such consultancies will be.

Appendix: Terms of Reference

1. The consultant is to undertake a comprehensive study of government employment. This will be preceded by a staff audit at central and local government levels to substantially reduce or wherever possible eliminate casual labor and temporary staff;

2. To examine *all* posts in order to determine whether they are essential to the provision of the *current level of services* or a reduced level of services is deemed sufficient;

3. To examine the level of expenditure on vehicles, equipment, drugs, services required for each post that is considered *essential;*

4. To identify the training and skills required for the efficient discharge of the functions considered *essential;*

5. To advise on the remuneration levels necessary to attract and retain and motivate individuals with the resources likely to be available;

6. To submit proposals for a substantial reduction in the government wage bill through *reduction* in the number of established posts, vacant and nonvacant, and temporary appointees, without *prejudice to the efficiency of public* administration and having regard to the need to improve remuneration of essential staff;

7. To prepare a five-year program for the *restructuring* of the civil service;

8. To give immediate and direct policy advice with regard to the structure and functioning of the civil service. It is expected to provide a basis for policy decision and reorganization of the service and its methods of functioning in order to rectify known deficiencies and to make the service an effective instrument for the achievement of national objectives, and also set a framework for further detailed work at the technical and administrative levels;

9. To review the management structures/systems of all ministries in general and those of selected ministries (Health, Agriculture, Education, Works and Communications), in particular, and advise with a view to improving organization of work, communication, policy formulation, and coordination. In this connection, it may be noted that an externally funded project for the health sector includes a management study of the health sector and it is expected that the proposals for the

reorganization of the Ministry of Works and Communications (especially its maintenance functions) will be reviewed in the context of the proposed externally funded highway maintenance project;

10. In consultation with the Institute for Management Development and the central personnel office, to review the management needs of the higher echelons of the civil service and make appropriate recommendations for the improvement of their training;

11. In consultation with the President's office and the central personnel office, to review the prospective role of the new Institute for Management Development in the training of public administrators, both executive and nonexecutive;

12. To review the pay policy with a view to promoting professionalism in the civil service, obtaining high-quality top management, and providing adequate incentives for efficient performance of public duties at all levels;

13. To review the present grading system on the basis of job evaluation criteria based on the following:

    • the work performed or to be performed,
    • the quality of performance,
    • the principle of equal pay for equal work,
    • comparable pay levels in the economy, and
    • budgetary resources available to government;

14. To develop a unified grading structure for the civil service;

15. To undertake, with the possible aid of appropriate grading teams, the regrading of all posts in the civil service on the basis of the new grading structure, establish scales of salaries corresponding to such grades, and, as a result of job evaluation of posts, recommend a salary scale applicable to each post in the service;

16. To review the position and make recommendations with regard to recruitment, promotion, training, and career management within the service, and mobility in and out of the service;

17. To review the role of the central management unit (central personnel office) in directing and running the service on a continuing basis;

18. To review and, if need be, revise the project for strengthening the central personnel office and advise on arrangements for its early implementation;

19. To assist in the selection of counterpart staff to serve under the above project and advise on their training program.

Notes

1. Milan Kubr, ed., *Management Consulting*, 2d ed. (Geneva: ILO, 1986), p. 467.

2. Kubr, *Management Consulting*, pp. 60–61.

3. Kubr, *Management Consulting*, p. 15.

4. Tudor Rickards, *Problem-Solving through Creative Analysis* (London: Gower Press, 1975), p. 55.

CHAPTER 9

The Reporting and Review Process in Consulting Assignments: How to Ensure Its Effectiveness

JAMES NTI

Many managers turn to consultants because they believe that such consultants will help them solve some nagging problems and bring about changes that will improve the health and, consequently, the performance of their organizations. As Kubr puts it, "organizational excellence is a common super-ordinate goal of management consulting. Consultants help to nudge organizations towards excellence."[1]

It is, however, common knowledge that a number of very good consultants' reports produced at high cost have ended up buried in the desks of clients without any hope of their ever being implemented. In many cases, this situation arises because during the consulting assignment an effective consultant-client relationship—a true collaborative relationship characterized by a shared desire to make the assignment succeed—has not been created and maintained. It is well known that human systems often resist, and in fact at times even reject, changes that are proposed from outside, however good they may be. Therefore, new changes stand the best chance of being implemented and becoming effective if they enjoy the support of the people concerned. Such support can be achieved only if those concerned have been given a chance to participate actively in all stages of the change effort. They must be able to claim ownership of the change or at least feel that they have contributed to the changes proposed.

How to Involve Clients in Consulting Assignments

Some consultants persist in adopting the traditional role of a consultant: an expert who has been engaged to provide a unique service because of his or her special knowledge, skill, and professional experience. Such consultants tend to take the directive approach and expect their clients to accept whatever they say in the false belief that their clients are incapable of fully appreciating what is good for their organizations. Consequently, after the initial contact meetings with their clients, they tend to proceed on their own, do the preliminary diagnosis of the organization's problems by themselves, collect the requisite information, analyze such information, and then submit a report that they expect to be implemented. They later come to realize to their chagrin that they have been living in a fool's paradise.

The dialogue between the consultant and the client that began during the initial contact meetings should be maintained throughout the assignment. For instance, it is very important that the client be fully involved in the diagnosis of the problems so that both client and consultant can clarify the goals of the consultancy assignment and the methods to be adopted in measuring such an achievement. By closely collaborating with the client in this exercise, the consultant sets in motion the process of attitudinal change.

It is also necessary to keep the client fully and regularly informed of the progress of the assignment. Providing the client with feedback at every stage of the assignment is extremely important if the consultant is to prevent negative attitudes and reactions on the part of the client. These negative feelings normally develop as a result of the client not being properly informed of what is going on. When the consultant's findings and conclusions come as a surprise, the initial response is usually resistance.

The information fed back to the client should "not just [be] any useful information but information collected, analyzed and selected by the consultant while working with the client."[2] In other words, such information should tell the client something new and important about the organization and the progress that is being made in finding solutions to the organization's problems. It should also be information that is likely to provoke the client to express reactions and thereby indicate to the consultant whether he or she is on the right track. Such information needs to be properly selected and presented, indicating any linkages there may be between the pieces of information and the causes of the organization's problems or the strengths and weaknesses of the organization. However, every effort should be made not to evaluate the client or make value judgements. The aim of consultants in giving feedback is to carry the client with them in the search for the appropriate solutions to the organizations' problems.

In some cases, the nature of the assignment determines the form in which the feedback is given. The two common forms of feedback are oral feedback given to individuals or to groups (at meetings) and written information in the form of interim reports or memoranda.

Reporting Periods

Feedback should be given when it can best contribute to the achievement of the overriding purpose. For instance, it should be given when the consultant wants to move from one stage of the assignment to another—for example, from data collection to data analysis—or when the analysis of the data indicates new and unenvisaged directions.

For a number of reasons, a useful time to give feedback is after the data-analysis stage. First, by reviewing the main findings with clients, consultants may be able to identify any gaps in their analysis. Second, such an exercise ensures that the conclusions that may be presented later will not come as a surprise to a client. Third, it serves as a means of seeking a client's agreement on whatever scheme the consultant has in mind to ensure the better functioning of the organization in the future.

In some consultancy contracts, the reporting periods are stipulated; in others, they are not. Whether such provisions are made in the contract or not, it is in the interest of consultants, if they wants their recommendations to be implemented and not buried in people's desks, to ensure that they gives regular feedback to clients at strategic stages of the assignment.

Defining the Client

When it comes to giving feedback, opinions are divided among consultants as to the definition of "the client." Some believe that feedback should be given only to selected individuals or to a small group of senior managers from whom the consultant can obtain help or action related to the particular problem. Others believe that such a definition is too restrictive, since in every consultancy assignment a consultant needs the assistance of a large number of people. Consequently, the consultant may feel obliged to share findings with all those who helped in data collection in order to to keep their goodwill.

Although such a debate may be interesting theoretically, in practice, consultants tend to give feedback to only a limited number of individuals who are directly or principally interested in the outcome of the assignment because of their responsibility for ensuring the proper functioning of the organization. In some cases, consultants find themselves restricted by the confidential nature of some information or even of the assignment itself.

Importance of the Feedback System to Consultants

Feedback is as important to the consultant as it is to the client. Besides using feedback as a technique to ensure the client's continued involvement in the consulting assignment, consultants also use feedback in other ways:

1. To obtain reactions on the investigative approach they are using in carrying out the assignment;

2. To identify gaps in their knowledge of the organization and obtain additional information;

3. To enable them to review both their approach and their line of search or hypothesis; and

4. To help them focus on key issues whose proper handling would improve the organization's performance.

How to Ensure the Effectiveness of the Reporting and Review Process

The effectiveness of the reporting and review process depends on a number of factors. For the consultant, these include the type of information given when reporting, the timing of reports, how the information is presented, and how the ensuing discussion is handled. For the client, factors that contribute to the effectiveness of this process include assigning appropriate individuals to monitor the consulting assignment and ensuring that such persons make adequate time available for the reporting and review process. Each of these factors is briefly discussed below.

The Consultant's Role

As discussed earlier, information that is reported to the client during the conduct of the consultancy assignment should tell the client something new about the problem under consideration. It should also be information that is likely to evoke reactions from the client. This implies that the information included in reports should be carefully selected by the consultant.

The timing of the reports is also important—at times, crucial. The consultant is not just reporting on work performed but is giving significant information to the client and should not treat the reporting exercise as routine. Consultants should ensure at the time of negotiating that scheduling of reports is properly done and that times stipulated in the consulting contract enable the reporting exercise to serve specific purposes. Furthermore, provision should be made in such contracts for flexibility, so the consultant can give feedback on significant developments that occur between scheduled reports. Consultants should also be free to articulate plans for change whenever they consider the time especially suitable.

The manner in which the information is fed back to the client can make a lot of difference in the effectiveness of the reporting and review process. The purpose of reports is not to evaluate the client or to impress the client per se. Thus it is not in good taste to harp on problems and difficulties being encountered or on the consultant's achievements during the reporting period. The presentation should be done in an impartial manner. This is particularly important when the consultant wishes to propose a new scheme as a substitute for the existing one. In such cases, the consultant should present, in some detail, both the positive and negative aspects of the two schemes and then sum up by drawing conclusions resulting from the comparison, indicating why the new proposed scheme is superior to the existing one. Such a comprehensive presentation normally weakens resistance to change and answers in advance some pertinent questions that might have been raised by the client. This is an application of the well-known management maxim that states, if you want someone to agree, make it easy for her or him to say yes. The consultant should be creative in arranging the knowledge gained and be able to develop conceptual models to explain or relate certain situations.

When presenting reports, consultants should make every effort to exude and gain trust. They must demonstrate that they are sincerely interested in helping the client. Managers who call in consultants are not fools; they can quickly discern whether a consultant is being objective and honest.

Although reports can be given orally, a proposal for a new scheme should be submitted in writing so that the client can read it and reflect upon it before the oral presentation is made by the consultant. This ensures that meaningful discussions can take place and that the consultant obtains the feedback needed to proceed with the assignment.

This points up the importance of being able to handle the discussions that follow the presentation in a skillful manner. Consultants are not reporting for the sake of reporting, they want to obtain some benefits from the exercise such as filling in gaps in their knowledge and, more importantly, getting reactions to their findings and direction. It is very much a process of self-appraisal—stopping and looking at how they are doing and getting the client, through comments and questions, to let them know how they might improve upon their performance. It is considered a crucial part of the consultant's role to use appropriate methods to elicit feedback.

In this connection, the consultant needs to exercise a lot of patience. Many consultants have learned that helping a client find solutions to problems can be a long and confrontational, if not daunting, experience, particularly when there is a difference in the cultural backgrounds of the client and the consultant. If some members of the client organization think that they may be adversely affected by the proposed changes they are likely to respond to such schemes with resistance, resentment, and deliberate interference. The consultant should be mature and realistic enough to recognize that some proposals are going to be thwarted. He must avoid reacting to disparaging comments with the defeatism and withdrawal that often accompany the frustration of a person's sincere efforts to help.

Obtaining the reactions of clients becomes a worthwhile exercise only when such feedback is used to reexamine hypotheses, investigative approaches, and analytical methods. In other words, such feedback should serve as a basis for review on the part of the consultant with a view to changing direction if necessary. Occasionally, the whole consulting assignment may be reviewed because information presented by the consultant indicates the existence of some new and maybe more important problems that were not foreseen at the initial stages of the consultancy assignment.

The Client's Role

It is important that both the client and the consultant approach the reporting or feedback sessions with the seriousness they deserve. Some clients have set up task forces or monitoring committees made up of highly esteemed persons in the organization to monitor the consulting assignment and how it is being carried out. These bodies can also act as sounding boards, thereby enabling consultants to get quick reactions to their proposals and approaches.

Whether such bodies are set up or not, it is important that clients make time available for receiving, reflecting upon, and reacting to the consultants' periodic reports. If such reports come in written form, clients should ensure that they are carefully read and considered before the consultant's oral presentation. During the presentation session clients should listen carefully to consultants to ensure that they do not miss any important statements and that they can live comfortably with the proposals being made. Clients should make every effort to communicate their reactions frankly and as precisely as possible.

Conclusion

Consulting involves people dealing with people. Both consultants and clients should, therefore, aim at achieving effective communication and at dealing with one another in an atmosphere of tact, trust, politeness, and stability.

Consultants are usually called in when clients are faced with what to them are puzzling and difficult situations. Resolving such situations is essentially a creative process. Normally there are no pat, textbook-type solutions; every consultancy assignment has its own peculiarities. Consultants can, therefore, make the reporting and review process effective by being imaginative and innovative and tailoring their concepts and behavior to the demands of the particular situation.

Notes

1. Milan Kubr, ed., *Management Consulting*, 2d ed. (Geneva: ILO, 1986), p. 214.
2. Kubr, *Management Consulting*, p. 163.

PART III

Institutional Experiences

CHAPTER 10

Experience as a Supplier of Management Consultancy in the Public Sector

Nigeria's Management Services and Training Department

ASON BUR

The thrust of this chapter is the problem of making optimal use of management consultants, particularly in Africa. I discuss it based on the experiences of my organization, the Management Services and Training Department (MSTD) of the Federal Civil Service Commission of Nigeria, as a public supplier of management consultancy services. The department occupies a unique position in that it must relate to management of the host organization as well as its counterparts from outside consulting organizations.

Management Consultancy Services

The definition of management consultancy given by the Institute of Management Consultants in the United Kingdom accurately describes the services of the MSTD. That institute defined management consultancy as:

the service provided by independent and qualified persons in identifying and investigating problems concerned with policy, organization, procedures and methods; recommending appropriate actions and helping to implement those recommendations.[1]

However, two considerations tend to challenge the appropriateness of that definition for the services the MSTD renders:

1. The exposure and, consequently, the professional skills of the MSTD's management consulting staff may appear to compare less favorably with those of their counterparts in the more advanced countries of the world; and

2. The MSTD is essentially a free "in-house" management consulting organ of the federal government of Nigeria. To that extent, its services are not rendered by an external organization that is absolutely independent of the chief client, the federal government

On the first consideration: The department's management consulting staff is, in relation to the assignments undertaken, highly exposed and skillful in specific, though limited, areas of the profession. Consequently, the department limits its intake of assignments to these identified areas.

On the second consideration: The MSTD is part of the Federal Civil Service Commission and works under its umbrella. From its inception, the independent status of the Federal Civil Service Commission has been guaranteed statutorily; that guarantee is entrenched in the Nigerian constitution. The MSTD is therefore independent of all the ministries, extraministerial departments, and parastatal institutions as well as state-owned companies. The MSTD is in a position to, and does, play an independent and impartial role in all internal management and operational problems in those organizations. This unique and central location of a public consultancy unit of government is necessary if it is to function properly and be given the attention and hearing it deserves.

Historical Development of Public-Sector Management Consultancy

The origins of the MSTD can be traced to a humble beginning in 1957, when the Ministry of Finance decided that the time was ripe to establish an Organization and Methods Unit (O & M Unit) in the Nigerian civil service. Thus in the 1958–59 fiscal year, the appropriate financial provisions were made by the Head of Estimates. Subsequently, in 1959, an adviser in organization and methods was seconded to the civil service of Nigeria from the United Kingdom to help set up the O & M Unit. By 1961, the unit was fully established under the leadership of an expatriate in the Nigerian civil service. The unit was relocated from the Finance Division of the Ministry of Finance to the Establishments Division of the then Ministry of Pensions and Service Matters, which later became known as the Federal Ministry of Establishments and Service Matters.

The main aim of the O & M Unit was to ensure that the various parts of the public service were as efficient as possible and that labor and materials were organized in a manner that left no room for waste. To achieve this aim, the unit was assigned specific duties, including the following:

- Analysis of methods and procedures

- Organizational analysis

- Records management

- Forms design and control

- General mechanization of office work

- Office planning and layout

- Clerical work measurement

Between 1960 and 1968, the O & M Unit carried out the above functions in various ministries and extraministerial departments in the federal civil service of Nigeria. It also published an "O & M Bulletin," which featured articles about general management and the management services function.

Because of the dearth of Nigerians in senior positions in the civil service at the time of its establishment, the O & M Unit was staffed at a relatively low level. But, following Wolle's report in 1968,[2] the unit was considerably improved and expanded through the injection of high-quality personnel drawn from both the administrative and professional classes in the civil service. Its staff members were given both local and overseas training, especially at the Royal Institute of Public Administration in London and at the U.S. Army Management Engineering Training Agency in Rock Island, Illinois.

In 1969, the functions of the O & M Unit were increased by the addition of the following:

- Administrative improvement of ministries and extraministerial departments

- Cost-benefit analysis

- Development of standard filing systems

- Workforce utilization

Following the 1974 report of the Public Service Review Commission,[3] which restructured the Nigerian public service, a new organ was created to implement the commission's recommendations. This new body, known as the Public Service Review Unit (PSRU), absorbed the O & M Unit. The PSRU was structured as follows:

- Management development and consultancy services section

- Compensation and salary policy section

- Grading operations section

- Pay research branch

A slight restructuring of the Nigerian civil service occurred in 1979[4] with the creation of the office of the Head of the Civil Service of the Federation. This office absorbed the host ministry of the PSRU and renamed the unit the Management Services Division, with the same structure as its predecessor. This designation was adopted to reflect its functions as an internal management consultancy unit in the federal public service.

The Establishment and Role
of the Management Services Division

The establishment of an in-house management consultancy unit in any organization is predicated on the need to have consultants readily available who can carry out the following functions:

- Continual review of existing administrative procedures and management practices, with a view to improving on those areas to attain higher efficiency and effectiveness;

- Introduction of new management techniques to keep abreast of the ever-changing business, political, and socio-economic environments within which the organization operates; and

- Liaison with external consultants and performance of joint assignments with them.

The establishment of the Management Services Division was a major reform in the federal public service of Nigeria, following the government's acceptance of the recommendations of the Public Service Review Commission under the chairmanship of Chief J. Udoji. Under the auspices of the office of the Head of the Civil Service of the Federation—the controlling and coordinating office of the entire civil service system—the Management Services Division was able to firmly establish itself as the government consulting unit and build up its credibility in order to enjoy acceptance among its numerous clients in the public service.

Initially, the major task of the division was to assist in implementing the Public Service Review Commission's recommendations that were accepted by the government, particularly in the areas of new management techniques and practices. In addition to continually reviewing the organizational structure of the civil service, the Management Services Division had the following specific functions:

- Install, on national basis, the new job evaluation system recommended by the Public Service Review Commission and approved by the government;

- Undertake additional job analysis and sampling required to complete the installation of the job evaluation system;

- Review and update, on a continuing basis, the entire job evaluation program so that new elements could be taken into account;

- Undertake a job grading audit to ensure that the approved grade levels were implemented by all organizations in the public service;

- Receive and investigate grading requests or petitions arising from disagreement with the job evaluation system; and

- Conduct pay surveys and analyze reports on its findings, and make recommendations on salaries and fringe benefits for the public service, including parastatals.

The Management Services Division carried out these functions and expanded its scope to include full-scale management consultancy services to all public-sector institutions. The government relied on its expert services and advice in making major decisions on proposals relating to the reorganization of ministries, departments, and parastatals. The division made full comments and recommendations to the government on new grading and personnel structures, training, and the implementation of a fringe benefits package. In addition, it carried out regular management and grading audits in the public service.

Creation of the Management Services and Training Department

In April 1988, new reforms were introduced into the Nigerian civil service.[5] The office of Head of the Civil Service of the Federation was eliminated. The Management Services Division and the Manpower Development Department in that office were grouped together to become the Management Services and Training Department, which now functions as one of the three departments of the Federal Civil Service Commission (FCSC). The MSTD is structured into the following divisions:

- Management consulting division

- Grading and staff inspection division

- Compensation policy and pay monitoring division

- Training division

Each division is headed by a deputy director who reports to a director who, in turn, reports to the director-general. The director-general reports to the chairman of the FCSC, who is the chief executive of the commission. With the demise of the office of Head of the Civil Service of the Federation, the FCSC is now the central agency with a coordinating and monitoring role.

In addition to its roles inherited from the O & M Unit and the PSRU, the management services component of the MSTD is required, under the ongoing Civil Service reforms, to "constantly review and propose modifications in the operational methods and organizational structure of the Civil Service."[6]

The training component is responsible for formulating training policy for the entire civil service and monitoring the execution of that policy. It is responsible for the management of six federal training centers, which train secretarial staff for the entire federal public service. It exercises a general supervision over the Administrative Staff College of Nigeria (ASCON) and monitors the implementation of a departmental training officers scheme, which established training units in all ministries and extraministerial departments. The training of training-unit staff is also its responsibility. The training division conducts the national secretarial diploma examination for those who wish to qualify as high-level secretarial personnel. In this connection, it inspects private secretarial institutions for their eligibility to prepare students for the national secretarial diploma examination. It also trains reporters for the twenty-one states and national assemblies as well as secretarial staff for statutory commissions established under the Nigerian constitution.

Impact of the MSTD
in Providing Consultancy Services

The entire federal public service constitutes the clientele of the Management Services and Training Department. There have been deliberate efforts on the part of the department and its predecessor, the Management Services Division, to increase the awareness of all public-sector institutions of the existence of its services and the role it can play in the development of management capability in the public service.

This reaching out to clients was achieved in the past by the periodic issuance of circulars that set forth the services the MSTD provides and also by articles in the now-defunct "Federal Newsletter,"[7] the in-house magazine of the federal civil service. Recommendations by past clients have also made prospective clients increasingly aware of the department's existence. The MSTD now markets its consultancy services by actually visiting clients in their home territories instead of relying on the above strategies. The previous, rather passive, approach paid off fairly well in the past, but it is inadequate in light of the current civil service reforms.

The MSTD has undertaken major organizational restructuring assignments in several key ministries, extraministerial departments, and parastatal institutions. In many cases, invitation letters have been personally signed by ministers, permanent secretaries (now redesignated directors-general), and general managers of parastatal institutions through their supervising ministries. Such clients include financial and transportation (railway and shipping) institutions.

However, many institutions in the public service have yet to make optimum use of the consulting services of the MSTD, especially in analyzing and finding solutions to the management problems they encounter in the course of their normal operations. In some cases, institutions remember that the services of this department are available only when they have proposals for reorganization, which are subject to critical review before government approval.

Part of the problem is that the number of management consulting staff in the department is inadequate to maintain contact with all the ministries, extraministerial departments, and parastatal organizations. It is partly in recognition of this inadequacy and partly because of the growing number of requests for assistance that the department is taking steps to recruit more staff of the right orientation, experience, and academic background within the public service. It has designed a training program that has both local and overseas components, including attachments to reputable practicing management consultancy organizations.

Establishment of Management Services Units in Ministries and Departments

It is government policy that Efficiency Units should be established in ministries and extraministerial departments. Such units are expected to carry out routine functions that will improve existing management and administrative procedures and gradually build up management's confidence in the competence of such units. Some steps have been taken to implement this policy, but it is too early to assess its effectiveness. It will take considerable time to recruit and train the staff, equip the units, and guide them toward realization of the aims for which they were established.

Relationship between the Training and Consulting Functions of the MSTD

The relationship between the two major functions of the department has been one of mutual support. The MSTD as a whole has one objective: the promotion of efficiency and effectiveness in the federal public service. As a consultancy unit, the staff of the management consulting division sometimes contributes to course inputs at the Administrative Staff College of Nigeria, which is under the general supervision of the MSTD. The consulting staff of the department runs courses, especially at junior and intermediate levels, for the staff of ministries and extraministerial departments. Such training is undertaken to support consultancy roles, and it is done in accordance with the training policy guidelines issued by the training division. Apart from monitoring the courses by departmental training officers, the management consulting division does not actually design and train staff of ministries and departments, so there is no clash of roles.

Interface between Public and Private Consultants

Before addressing the question of the interface between public-sector and private-sector consultants, it is necessary to explain what constitutes the public service. The Nigerian public service is made up of the following subsystems:

- The civil service, which encompasses the ministries and extraministerial departments;

- The armed forces;

- The police force;

- The parastatals and state-owned companies;

- Local government; and

- Educational institutions.

In the civil service, the MSTD is the only management consultancy unit that exists as an internal service organ within the system. It therefore has an almost exclusive market among the ministries and extraministerial departments in the purely management services duties it specializes in. The department's competence and authority in these areas have been established, and there is no competition with private-sector consultants. However, in the area of staff development, especially in terms of performance-improvement training courses for lower staff, some private consulting firms have been engaged by ministries and departments from time to time.

In the case of parastatals, there is, in principle, a free market: Consultants from both sectors can participate. However, such participation usually depends on the status of the parastatal and the type of assignment it generates. Parastatals that are noncommercial and are dependent on government funding are invariably within the grading system of the MSTD. In the case of the considerably autonomous and commercially oriented parastatals, the market appears to be a free-for-all in terms of competition. Here, the private management consultancy groups compete for jobs among themselves and often with the consultancy units of some public establishments such as ASCON, the Centre for Management Development, and the universities. The MSTD, however, has never engaged in competition with other consultants. Besides the fact that there is always work on hand from the ministries, the department is not commercially oriented and offers its services free to its clients. Nonetheless, some of the largely autonomous parastatals have often referred cases regarding management and personnel matters to the MSTD. This is to be expected, and the trend is healthy for the development of both public and private consultancy and its utilization in Nigeria.

Crisis of Acceptability

It is my strong belief that the roles of the public and private suppliers of consultancy services are fully complementary. But it seems, from experience, that this complementarity has not been fully appreciated by either side.

Some private consultants have the erroneous idea that public officers, by the nature of their functions, cannot act as management consultants. Public-sector consultants argue that private consultants have not had sufficient training in any specialized areas of management consultancy. I call this the crisis of acceptability. These attitudes create an unhealthy rivalry between the two different suppliers of consultancy services to the detriment of the organizations they are supposed to serve.

To tackle this problem, the staff of the MSTD participates in workshops and seminars in which both parties meet to exchange ideas. For example, the MSTD held a one-week seminar on human resource development and utilization in Nigeria, the aim of which was to formulate a policy in this vital area. Many private-sector consultants and top managers were invited to participate in the seminar—and they did so enthusiastically.

The MSTD is a corporate member of the Nigerian Association of Management Consultants, a body that admits both private- and public-sector consultants. Many staff members of the department are also members of the Nigerian Institute of Management and the Nigerian Institute of Personnel Management. Consultants from the private sector belong to these groups as well. So, gradually but steadily, we are building bridges and reaching out for mutual cooperation and understanding.

Furthermore, the MSTD is intensifying the training of its consultants in modern management techniques to enable them to play the role of "doctor" to sick organizations by diagnosing and effectively treating their ills.

Crisis of Credibility

The question of the credibility of consultants is a major problem facing the industry today, in both the public and private sector. The establishment of management services units in ministries and departments is one way in which the MSTD is tackling the credibility problem. The department also believes that the credibility of a consulting organization depends on the caliber of its personnel, so it emphasizes the training and retraining of its management consultants.

The MSTD also ensures that its staff acquires experience by means of both attachments to relevant organizations and guided assignments. The department believes that if it recruits people with good personality, experience, and the requisite qualities and attributes, it should be able to avert crises arising from gaps in credibility and acceptability.

Crisis of Effectiveness

In the West African subregion, the training of consultants and the utilization of their services have generally been given low priority by the governments, which make little budgetary provision for consultancy services. I refer to this situation as the crisis of effectiveness.

In my own organization, the MSTD, I insist that each division head draw up a comprehensive annual training program for her or his staff. Such programs must show the correct financial implications, which must be defended effectively in order to receive the necessary approval. Either I or my director leads the delegation of department representatives when it goes to the appropriate government agency to defend the annual budget proposal. Using this strategy, we have been able to get reasonable budgetary provisions for staff training and development.

I believe that the efficiency of the supporting junior staff—including messengers, secretaries and clerical staff—plays a role in the overall efficiency of the senior staff. This is my philosophy regarding the coverage of training programs and, in my capacity as director-general, I preach it to my senior officials.

Today's managers, in both the private and public sectors, have the task and responsibility of molding the future of any given nation. Whether we sink or swim is determined by the types of decisions made by this group. Their effectiveness depends solely on their integrity, dynamism, creativity, depth of knowledge, and the courage to make right decisions. All these attributes can be obtained mainly through orientation or training.

What should be emphasized is that every organization—big or small, public or private—depends on a core or pool of managerial talents for its continued survival and development. For consultancy to thrive and make an impact, training in the field must be accorded a higher priority and given adequate funding. Adequate attention must also be given by our training institutions to character profile, administrative and personal skills, intellectual ability, and stability of performance, in addition to professional training. Only this can create institutionalization of management integrity and ethics.

Scope and Limits of
Management Consultancy in the Public Service

As discussed earlier, the consultancy functions and roles assigned to the Management Services and Training Department are limited to structural organizations, management techniques, job analysis and classification, grading and wages, and cooperation with similar consultancy bodies inside and outside the government.

These functions are evaluative—relevant, but routine. What is more, they do not emphasize the need for efficiency and productivity. These factors are especially important in Third World countries, where governments are directly involved—and, in some cases, play dominant roles—in major economic programs and projects traditionally reserved for the private sector.

The public productive sector of the economy is generally supervised by bureaucrats who, in the critical eyes of the public, are inefficient and dishonest, and are therefore incapable of satisfying societal expectations. Such criticisms are hardly contestable in light of how some of our public-sector enterprises—for example, hotels, transportation, hospitals, electricity, airways, and schools—are run and supervised by public officers. I call this situation the crisis of confidence and effective deliverance.

Those consulting to the public sector need to possess those skills that make rapid economic development and transformation possible. They must have the necessary technological and scientific competence. Bureaucratic consultants should be willing to use the services of private-sector consultants to achieve the desired results. Consultancy in the public and private sectors must cooperate—pull available resources and expertise together to ensure that common goals are realized. Public and private consultants should work together, giving priority to the planning capabilities of the public sector, of which private-sector planning is an extension. To facilitate this, several objectives are necessary:

- To upgrade training techniques and incentives;

- To reduce red tape in government and increase efficient and profitable processes of decisionmaking;

- To improve the effectiveness of services to the public sector and complement the development process;

- To facilitate the smooth running of public organizations through a review of establishment principles;

- To minimize discrepancies and remove excessive controls to enable the effective implementation of public-sector programs;

- To establish forums such as associations, seminars, workshops, and conferences through which consultants in the public and private sectors can meet to exchange views and enrich their experiences; and

• To define and redefine the scope of management consultancy, develop a code of ethics, and enhance the development of the industry.

Conclusion

There is no doubt that Africa and the Third World in general need to develop their own capabilities and programs to attain self-reliance and rapid economic growth. The economic necessities of the times have forced public and private organizations to resort to fundamental restructuring and reorganizations of varying complexities. These are aimed at overcoming existing problems and achieving effective and maximum utilization of the scarce resources available. Management consultancy, no doubt, has a crucial role to play in this transformational stage. Fortunately for the profession, the needs mentioned above have increased the awareness and use of consultants in various fields of development. What we need to do to ensure optimal utilization is to recount, refine, and add to the strategies we adopted in the Management Services and Training Department of the Federal Civil Service Commission of Nigeria.

Notes

1. M. Kubr, ed., *Management Consulting: A Guide to the Profession* (Geneva: ILO, 1976), p. 7.
2. C. P. Wolle, *Training Needs of the Federal Civil Service—A Survey* (Lagos: Federal Ministry of Information, Printing Division, 1968), pp. 78–87.
3. Main Report: *The Public Service Review Commission* (Lagos: Federal Ministry of Information, Printing Division, 1974).
4. Section 157(2)(3) of the Constitution of the Federal Republic of Nigeria, 1979.
5. Presidential Task Force on the Implementation of the Civil Service Reforms, *Main Report and Summary Recommendations* (Lagos: Federal Government Printer, 1988).
6. Presidential Task Force, *Main Report*, p. 15, ¶10.3.
7. "Federal Civil Service Newsletter," no. 11 (May 1977), pp. 2, 8.

CHAPTER 11

Consultancy Services at ESAMI: Past Experiences and Future Prospects

TALALA MBISE AND P. S. P. SHIRIMA

This chapter describes the consultancy services offered by the Eastern and Southern African Management Institute (ESAMI). It provides a brief historical background and general profile of the institute, presents the general framework of ESAMI's consultancy services, and discusses the consulting experience of ESAMI.

Background

Establishment and Membership

ESAMI was established in 1974 at Arusha, Tanzania, as the East African Management Institute (EAMI) under the sponsorship of the three partner states in the East African Community (EAC): Kenya, Tanzania, and Uganda. EAMI was originally conceived as a management development center offering training, consultancy, and research services to organizations (private and public) in the EAC. After the breakup of the EAC, the partner governments decided to convert EAMI into ESAMI. The new institute was formalized through the signing of an agreement establishing it at a conference of plenipotentiaries held at Arusha, Tanzania, on 28 February 1980.

Membership in ESAMI is open to all states of the Eastern and Southern African subregion, namely: Angola, Botswana, Comoros, Djibouti, Ethiopia, Kenya, Lesotho, Madagascar, Malawi, Mauritius, Mozambique, Seychelles, Somalia, Swaziland, Tanzania, Uganda, Zambia, and Zimbabwe. These states constitute ESAMI's main service area.

Purpose and Objectives

The broad purpose of ESAMI is to improve the performance and management effectiveness of public and private institutions in the subregion. ESAMI does this by:

- Promoting, organizing, cosponsoring, and facilitating the organization of management training courses that are designed to improve the skills and performance of management personnel in the public (government), parastatal, and private institutions and enterprises within the member states.

- Serving as a specialized regional center for training, research, and consultancy in various management fields, with particular focus on the management of public enterprises. In addition, ESAMI seeks to test, evaluate, develop, and disseminate new techniques in the areas of financial management, transport and communications management, materials management, health services management, project management, human resources management, production management, and marketing.

- Undertaking, cosponsoring, or facilitating the conduct of studies on administrative, management, and organizational problems with respect to the socioeconomic and technological development of the member states.

- Providing documentation and information services and acting as a reference center in the field of management and providing management consultancy services to public and private institutions within its member states at their request.

- Collaborating with national, regional, and international management development institutions and associations in carrying out the above activities.

Major Activities

Training. ESAMI offers regional management training programs in various areas, including project planning and management, public finance and taxation, transportation and communications management, management of electronic data-processing systems, health services management, public enterprise management, production management and marketing, materials management, women in development, training of trainers, human resources management, and financial management and accounting. The programs are designed for middle, upper-middle, and top management executives in government and industry.

Over the past five years, ESAMI has designed, organized, and implemented an average of forty different management training courses a year, equivalent to 100 participant weeks per course. On average, 900 participants from organizations within the ESAMI service area (including those from nonmember states) have attended ESAMI training courses each year for the past five years.

ESAMI also provides tailor-made courses that are designed and conducted with the cooperation of client organizations to meet their specific needs. These courses are conducted either at ESAMI or on the premises of the client organization. They generally last from one to six weeks and have included such specialized areas as industrial relations, small industries development, corporate planning, production and operations management, financial management and accounting, marketing and sales promotion, electronic data processing, and programming and budgeting systems.

In the past five years, ESAMI has designed and conducted an average of fifteen tailor-made courses a year for various client organizations in various management areas. This is equivalent to an annual average of 970 participant weeks, or about 65 participant weeks per course per year. The parastatal sector has been the major client for tailor-made courses.

Consultancy. Consultancy is another of ESAMI's management development functions. It assists clients in solving operational, administrative, and management problems. Details are presented later in this chapter.

Research. In addition to training and consultancy functions, ESAMI carries out applied research activities either on request from client organizations (including government agencies and international organizations) or at its own initiative as part of its efforts to develop training materials and contribute to the growth of baseline knowledge in the field of management.

Organization, Administration, and Staffing

ESAMI is an intergovernmental organization with a governing board composed of one representative from each member state. The representatives are nominated by their respective governments on the basis of management expertise and relevant experience. Representatives of international, regional, and private business organizations and universities participate in the board's activities from time to time.

ESAMI is administered on behalf of the governing board by a director-general who is, in turn, assisted by a deputy director-general. Senior administrative responsibilities are carried out by a registrar and a financial officer. A senior librarian administers the library and documentation center. At the present time, there are thirty-five full-time consultants allocated to seven divisions organized around major training emphases and consultancy. ESAMI's full-time staff members serve under three-year renewable contracts. They are derived exclusively from nationals of the member states and are selected solely on the basis of professional qualifications and demonstrated competence.

Finance

ESAMI is largely self-financing. Fees charged for its services make it generally self-supporting. ESAMI receives only about 10 percent of its budget in the form of subventions from member governments.

Support from International Donors. In addition to support from member governments, ESAMI attracts substantial support for its programs. About thirty international donor agencies have contributed in one way or another to ESAMI's programs, in the form of grants of equipment, provision of staff, or scholarships.

ESAMI'S Consultancy Function

The Mandate

ESAMI and its predecessor, EAMI, have provided consultancy services to member government agencies and to public and private enterprises in the subregion since 1974. Until two to three years ago, consultancy services occupied an average of 5 to 10 percent of ESAMI's professional staff time, not counting time spent on the tailor-made training programs referred to earlier. Based on the projected demand for ESAMI consultancy services, the management of ESAMI is currently implementing a program to strengthen the consulting function. It is:

1. Establishing a full-time consultancy division with a core team of consultants in order to institutionalize what was formerly a committee function;

2. Establishing collaborative arrangements with organizations (internal and external to the subregion) that have similar interests as ESAMI;

3. Providing for use of technical assistance to complement, supplement, and develop internal expertise; and

4. Recognizing consultancy as a high potential revenue earner for the institute.

Purpose and Objectives

The primary purpose of ESAMI's consultancy services is to provide assistance to government agencies and to public and private enterprises in the ESAMI service area, complementing and supplementing ESAMI's mission of performance improvement.

The key objective of ESAMI's consulting mission is to provide client organizations with professional assistance in the use and development of internal and external resources for diagnosing, redesigning, and implementing organizational systems and structures aimed at improving management systems performance. The primary focus at the present time is on institutional capacity building and sustainability.

Operational Assumptions

The supply of ESAMI's consultancy services is guided by the following assumptions based on a long consulting experience in the region:

- There is a direct relationship among training, consultancy, and applied research.

- Demand for consultancy services is normally based on the need to achieve important and lasting improvements by the use of expertise that the client organization could not permanently sustain.

- An organizational performance improvement exercise initiated through consultant services may have lasting results only if it is operationally sustainable.

- An operationally sustainable improvement is possible only if it is complemented and supplemented by the corresponding development of institutional capacity.

- Conventional (that is, academic) approaches to supply of consultancy services are least effective in sub-Saharan Africa.

- The problem expressed by the client should not be diagnosed separately from the client's operating environment. And since the client has a better understanding of the operating environment, an effective consultant is one who is willing to play the role of "mobilizer" or "partner" in the process of supplying the consultancy service.

- Most organizational failures in sub-Saharan Africa—especially in the ESAMI service area—have resulted from not only the inadequacy of management skills but also from ill-conceived processes of organizational design.

ESAMI's Consultancy Method

Conventional Methods

In the past, and at the request of a client, ESAMI has used conventional approaches to diagnose and redesign organizational systems and structures aimed at improving management systems performance. The basic model in the conventional approach is the "consultant engineering" model or its close surrogate. Using this model, a consultant provides the client with complete technical assessments and specifications in the form of recommendations.

The advantages of the conventional approach to consultancy include the following:

- It is time efficient;

- It is cost saving;

- Quality and quantity of technical or substantive results meet "standard" requirements; and

- The resulting judgment is independent of client management biases.

Experience has revealed that use of the conventional approach, especially in management and organizational areas, results in the design of systems that:

- Fail miserably, are poorly implemented, are discontinued and forgotten, or impose unacceptably large burdens on organizational resources;

- Are process inefficient and costly in the long run;

- Are often unrealistic, nonoperational, and unimplementable, and result in systems improvement goals that are unattainable;

- Make assumptions about the organization's environment; and

- Rarely produce a lasting impact on the organization's capacity to sustain itself.

Process Consultancy Approach

Based on the inadequacies of the conventional approach as well as on its experience in the service area, ESAMI has recently adopted the process consultancy approach to the supply of consultancy services. With this approach, ESAMI works *with* rather than *for* the client right from the problem definition stage through the implementation of the solution. In the process, risks are shared through a jointly agreed formula. At the end of the process, a client not only implements a solution it developed, but has also developed the internal capacity to carry out similar exercises within the organization with minimal external assistance.

In ESAMI's judgment, which is based on experience in at least seven countries in Africa (six in the ESAMI service area and one in West Africa), process consultancy is the most effective approach in sub-Saharan Africa. Indeed, various donors and donor agencies including the World Bank, the International Fund for Agricultural Development (IFAD), the U.S. Agency for International Development (USAID), and the Canadian International Development Agency (CIDA) have initiated or used a similar process at various stages of project development in several African countries and elsewhere.

ESAMI'S Consulting Experience

Demand for ESAMI Consultancy Services

In the past three to four years, ESAMI has successfully carried out more than twenty different consultancy projects in seven different countries in the subregion. About 20 percent of these were secured from governments, and 70 percent were secured from parastatals (public enterprises). The rest were secured from the private and the nongovernment sectors.

At the time of this writing, there are two ongoing consultancy projects, including one that was competitively secured from an international nongovernmental organization based in Geneva. In addition, five consultancy projects are in the final securing stages in three different countries in the subregion. All are in the parastatal sector. Four consultancy projects are in the pipeline (not guaranteed) in three different countries in the subregion.

Staff Development

In the past two years, ESAMI has allocated the equivalent of about five full-time staff members to consulting services because of growing demand. Before that it allocated an average of only two.

About 80 percent of the requests for ESAMI consultancy services have been in the areas of management and design, corporate planning, and management development. The rest have been in the area of specialized technical assessments of an engineering type, for example, transport construction and project studies. Thus, judging from past requests for ESAMI consultancy services, the majority of client problems that create the need for consultancy assistance are in the area of general management and organizational systems.

Market Potential

Assume that each of the eighteen member countries of ESAMI has ten government agencies and ten parastatal organizations, each of which has one problem requiring the full-time services of one ESAMI consultant for two weeks a year. That would be equivalent to a fourteen-member full-time consulting staff. Clearly, ESAMI would not have the capacity, at present levels of allocation, to satisfy the demand.

Ironically, there is presently an excess consultancy capacity at ESAMI by an average of 30 to 40 percent. The key issue is, why? In order to resolve the issue, there is need to look at both the behavior and characteristics of consultancy service demand and supply in the African region in general, and the ESAMI service area in particular.

Opportunities, Problems, and Constraints

Currently, ESAMI could allocate about 30 to 50 percent of its overall internal professional staff capacity to consultancy services without necessarily disrupting its training, research, and publications activities.

Over 95 percent of the ESAMI professional staff have been recruited from the ESAMI service area. Thus, they have the requisite experience in and thorough knowledge of the area. They also have the most comprehensive stock of skills to serve the consultancy requirements of the area.

ESAMI has established country and subregional offices in Dar es Salaam, Harare, Nairobi, and Entebbe to effectively promote and market ESAMI's consultancy, training, research, and publications services. Each office has a permanent resident position for a professional consultant whose major duties include establishing ESAMI activity links in the respective country or subregion.

The current trend is for donor-recipient relationships to be forged through regional or subregional organizations. ESAMI is in a far better position to serve that linkage role, both substantively and in terms of process effectiveness. For example, major bilateral and multilateral agencies have expressed a preference for technical assistance in the ESAMI service area to be provided through ESAMI. Chances are good that this behavior could be institutionalized.

To take advantage of donor trends as well as to complement and supplement its consultancy services, ESAMI has been registered and accredited in the European Economic Community (EEC) and other donor-source countries. It has also entered into collaborative and joint agreements with regional and international consulting organizations within and outside the ESAMI service area, including North America and Europe.

The major problems that ESAMI faces in the supply of consultancy services in the subregion include the following:

- *Client attitudes, legacy, and experience.* In general, clients in the ESAMI service area in particular, and Africa in general, have tended to award consultancy contracts to international organizations based outside Africa. The basic attitude has been: "What can a fellow African tell me that I do not know? After all, we went to the same school." There are two ways to interpret this attitude: The positive way is as a recognition of the need to transfer skills from outside one's own operating environment; the negative way is as the judgment of ideas based on origin rather than competence.

- *Information and marketing.* More often than not, clients in the ESAMI service area do not have adequate information on internally or regionally available consultancy service—its quality, cost, and potential. Consequently, they cannot choose what they are not aware of.

- *Donor requirements.* In some cases, the financing of a consultancy project may be tied to donor conditions. Relevant examples include "Title Twelve" and ICB. The former restricts "entry," and the latter imposes competitive constraints based on noncomparable environments.

- *Budgetary constraints.* Quality consultancy service is expensive. A majority of clients rarely budget or provide for the use of consultancy services except when a client's financier provides for it.

Conclusions

At the present time, the use and supply of consultancy services in the ESAMI service area are financed primarily through donors and donor agencies, but there is no guarantee that this behavior will continue forever. Individual clients must identify and budget for consultancy service requirements. Consultancy service suppliers need to be much more aggressive in marketing themselves.

Conceptually, and on the basis of experience, the process consultancy approach is considered, at least at the present, to be the most effective approach in the ESAMI service area and perhaps in the developing world as a whole.

The focus of the supply and demand of consultancy services should be in the areas of management and information systems, organizational development and design, corporate planning, management development, and project studies.

Reliance on external consultants is unlikely to lead to long-term, sustainable solutions to organizational and management problems within the African environment. Internal, regional, and subregional consulting capabilities need to be developed as well. The best and tested method for building the capacity for the maintenance of organizational and management systems is the process consultancy approach, in which ESAMI has proved its competence.

CHAPTER 12

Optimal Utilization of Consultants: ASCON's Perspective

MIKE B. DURODOLA

A discussion of the utilization of consultancy in Africa inevitably has to deal with an examination of how the profession can be most effective in facilitating national and continental economic and social development in a modern setting.

Africa's broad developmental process requires many things, among which are:

- The basic human, physical, and financial resources;

- A framework of government policies and plans that are favorable to growth, including monetary, fiscal, and trade policies; plans for education; and the provision of infrastructural needs; and

- A national attitude or a national aspiration—in the people themselves—that growth and development are desirable.

Another requirement is the means for knowledge transfer—probably both from external sources to the domestic economy and within the domestic economy itself. With the increasing desire of African nations to gain modern technology, the importance of the knowledge-transfer function has become more apparent. It is in this knowledge-transfer function that consultancy finds its role.

Consultancy and Socioeconomic Development

Management consultancy is a service that is geared toward bringing about change. It is a catalytic function in a nation's growth and development process. It is, or can be, the instrument that brings together the separate ingredients of the process and induces, or produces, dynamic change so that development will, in fact, occur.

When we look at the total contemporary environment of the African continent, we see the problems of inflation and the uncertainties surrounding world and continental trading relationships, resulting from the fragility of the international monetary situation. We also see the problems that have flowed from the energy crisis and the problem of raw material and commodity shortages of an unprecedented scale. There are other problems: the need to improve efficiency, the lack of regard for workers as individual human beings, environmental damage, and the concern that economic processes should serve social and not purely private ends.

It is this scenario that appears to require the increasing use of consultants in Africa. Consultants bring together experts in various disciplines relevant to the needs of client organizations. This, however, requires that such consultants always be up-to-date on the latest developments in their disciplines. Working from the position of independence, consultants are ideally placed to conduct expert analyses and give objective advice to client organizations whose management could not ordinarily afford to devote full-time attention to narrow specializations, would not have the time to conduct in-depth analyses, and does not possess the objectivity of a dispassionate observer. The accumulated experience of consultants acquired from wide-ranging organizations also constitutes a reservoir of knowledge and skills that can favorably influence organizational performance.

The Prevailing Context of
Management Consultancy Practice in Africa

Management consultants in Africa practice under conditions that do not exactly replicate those prevailing in developed countries. Consequently, their contributions and effectiveness can be validly assessed only on the basis of the objectives, motivations, and impelling and impending forces that are pertinent to the African situation. Implied in this suggestion is that there is some relationship between the management consultant and the environment. This nexus is inevitably one that will ensure relevance, purposeful development, and the optimum impact of effort on results.

Another distinct implication of this relationship is the methodological approach it imposes. What readily comes to mind is the doctor-patient relationship. Like a medical doctor, the management consultant is often called in to treat organizational ailments. In doing this, the consultant bears in mind not only the problems prevailing within the client organization but also the fact that as an organ of society, the organization is part of a wider environment that is characterized by certain general tendencies and responds to more or less the same stimuli and pressures. For a successful intervention, therefore, the management consultant has to approach his work with basically the same stimuli, pressure, and methodological framework as the medical doctor.

Africa is at present beset with what may be described as the deepest economic recession it has ever experienced. All the important indicators of well-being, such as income levels, employment, availability of essential goods and services, and price affordability, have shown a consistent decline since the beginning of this decade, with no immediate prospect of a halt or recovery. This situation has, in turn, unleashed onto the general populace severe hardships, social ills, and stresses that manifest themselves in many discomforts and threats to life and property.

The prevailing situation constitutes the final outcome of a series of acts of omission or commission extending over the last two decades perpetrated not only by the political leadership and successive governments, but also by all those individuals in whatever positions they occupied whose responsibility impinged on management. Public-sector management has not been altogether sincere or purposeful in addressing the problems of the respective countries, nor has it demonstrated a high degree of competence in the management of the continent's resources. The planning of the economy is only paid lip service, resulting in excessive dependence on monocultural products, inability to sustain basic infrastructures, neglect of the agricultural sector in the face of a rapidly expanding population, and nonpolicy on the siting of economic projects.

Even management in the private sector falls below the required standard in certain aspects of professionalism. Here, management has usually shown a too-ready willingness to concede high professional standards and ethics—if not a sense of nationalism—in its efforts to win patronage and maximize profits. But the well-vaunted efficiency of private-sector management—often exemplified with high business profits and large annual turnovers—may be a function of both a reasonable amount of managerial diligence and a certain predisposition toward sharp business practices and indifference to, if not outright defiance of, the dictates of regional, subregional, and national interests. Such willingness to compromise professional standards and continental interests is at the root of many of the ills suffered by the management profession in Africa today.

The foregoing emphasizes the almost limitless opportunities for management consultants on the continent of Africa.

Client-Consultant Responsibilities

Like all other professions, consultancy has three main requirements. First, there must be a body of knowledge with which practitioners should be familiar and have access to in doing their job. Second, there must be minimum entry conditions. Third, the profession has to be guided by a code of professional conduct. A practitioner needs to exhibit these requirements; the user or client needs to be familiar with them so as to optimize the use of consultants.

Clients should know that management consultancy does not and cannot provide miracle solutions to difficult managerial problems. Many clients assume that once a consultant has been commissioned, life becomes easy for the organization. This is an illusion, and practitioners know it. Consulting is an often difficult but systematic work based on the analysis of facts and the search for imaginative and feasible solutions. Consequently, management commitment to solving organizational problems and client-consultant cooperation are just as important to the end result as the quality of the consultant's advice.

There is glamour in consultancy, both in its practice and in its use. Perhaps this induces clients to hire consultants for the wrong reasons; and once hired, the consultants are generally poorly utilized and loosely supervised. More satisfactory results from a consulting engagement can be obtained if the client uses common sense in making decisions about when to hire consultants, whom to hire, what the consultants are to do, and how they are to do it.

In order to optimize the use of consultancy, I suggest that hiring a consultancy service should be a last-resort solution for any project, particularly those in which the consultant is not to be a part executor. Hardheaded business or economic reasons should be the major factor in hiring consultants; they should be assigned responsibility for duties that, given the client's needs, it would be uneconomical, inefficient, and ineffective to do in-house.

However, once the decision has been made to engage a consultant, the client should take pains to screen the prospective consultant, seek clarification of how the consultant will operate, and ensure that the end products are clearly specified. The client should also explain resource limitations, define the consultant's role, and set performance, monitoring, and evaluation standards. The consultant must identify the "real" problems, specify his and the client's roles, and ensure that he adapts to the client's particular problems. In addition, the consultant must demonstrate competence and offer feasible and implementable solutions.

ASCON's Experience

Objectives

The Administrative Staff College of Nigeria (ASCON) came into existence in 1972. Its objectives, among others, were to provide higher management training for the development of senior executives for the public and private sectors of the economy and to undertake research and consultancy services. In order to meet the enormous and wide-ranging needs of the public sector, the college now combines the role of an administrative staff college with that of a civil service college. It undertakes both developmental training and job-related management training courses for all categories of public servants at grade level 08–16.

Apart from the regular courses, ASCON also organizes, on a consultancy basis, training in a number of unscheduled programs mounted at the request of clients in the various state capitals. The college is also engaged in designing, developing, and delivering series of consultancy and training programs aimed at enhancing the technical capability and capacity of officers involved in policy formulation, development, and promotion of small-scale industries in Nigeria. Examples of these new foci are:

- The Small and Medium Exterprises Consultancy Course (SAMECC), which develops participants' expertise in counseling and setting up prospective entrepreneurs; and

- The Working-for-Yourself Course, which literally teaches would-be small-scale industrialists how to start and succeed in business.

However, ASCON's activities are not confined to Nigerian national borders. The staff was involved in a series of seminars mounted for Zimbabwe senior public officials in 1981, and the College Management Consultancy Unit successfully carried out a survey of the training needs of the Zimbabwe civil service. The decision of the Zimbabwe government to establish a Zimbabwe Institute of Public Administration and Management (ZIPAM) was influenced by the recommendation of the final consultancy report.

Consultancy

ASCON has an institution-based consulting department that has responsibility for initiating, providing, and coordinating all college consultancy activities. Although the college engages the services of other consultants, the focus of the rest of the chapter is on the services that the college consultancy staff provides. ASCON supplies consultancy services mainly to public-sector organizations. The services cover:

- Organizational studies and reorganization;

- Commercialization of public enterprises;

- Training needs identification and training design and implementation;

- Feasibility studies;

- Project management;

- Supervision of other consultants; and

- Policy formulation.

Most of ASCON's consulting relationships were quite satisfactory, but not without the usual problems. There are the hassles and lobbying that go with bidding for public-sector jobs, and coping with the kickback expectations of some of the functionaries of the prospective client organizations. There is also the client's low level of awareness of the clear objectives of an assignment. In addition, there are the issues of disregard for competence, favoritism, and noncommitment of client personnel. There are also the problems related to monitoring and evaluating project performance.

Of course, the college does receive a lot of invitations to bid for assignments; indeed, most of the assignments it has executed resulted from its excellent proposals in response to such requests. However, because of ASCON's belief in, and commitment to, the promotion of the consultancy profession, as well as its regard for safeguarding the interests of prospective clients, it always ensures that it meets two standards:

1. Competence and capability in the problem or assignment area; and

2. Adherence to deadlines agreed on with clients.

ASCON believes in its mission of service to the nation and therefore devises ways and means for coping with most of the factors that could inhibit the effective performance of an assignment. In executing some assignments, ASCON has had to seek out collaborators for areas in which the college has limited capability. In doing that, the college disclosed their full identities to the clients right from the proposal stage. ASCON's associates were involved in all major discussions and negotiations with the clients. This enabled the college consultants and their associates to operate with the same frame of mind in executing the assignments. However, in my view, unless the client and the consultant mutually deal with the various problems I have enumerated, the ideal we seek in publishing this book will continue to elude us. When clients' awareness is high, it will be easy to demand the imposition of sanctions against erring consultants by the appropriate professional body.

Training of Consultants

As should already be evident, the greatest area of influence and impact of ASCON's consultancy department is training. The college offers specialized fifteen-week training courses in management consultancy for officers who are expected to function in the management consulting or management services units of their organizations. Unfortunately, posttraining evaluation has revealed that trained consultants in the public service rarely have the opportunity to use the knowledge and skills acquired during training. It appears that the issue of the relevance of job-related training has little or no meaning within the public service, which inhibits optimal utilization of consultancy knowledge and skills.

To minimize this problem, and in order to enhance the effectiveness of ASCON's training, it was strongly advocated that deployment of officers be tied to training in relevant, specific job-related areas. This problem assumed such a great dimension with participants in the college's management consultancy course that ASCON had to suspend the program until a definite decision was made on the appropriate deployment of the trained officers.

Conclusion

There is room for considerable improvement in the use of consultancy in Africa's continued search for economic and social development. But the best results can be achieved from consultants only if clients themselves are knowledgeable about the process, limitations, and expectations of consultancy and are willing to cooperate without influencing or inhibiting the consultant's objective and independent analysis and recommendations.

African indigenous consultants need to develop themselves through training and exposure or through attachments to highly reputable consulting firms, where they can acquire the necessary skills in process consulting. Through training and practical exposure to our cultural and management peculiarities, indigenous consultants would have the advantage in being able to critically analyze our organizational problems more objectively and would be in a better position to postulate more realistic and practicable recommendations. What is required is that every party—the client, the consultant, and consultancy regulating bodies—play its role. We need joint action, not buck passing—commitment rather than lip service.

CHAPTER 13

Setting Up and Operating an Internal Consultancy Facility

Experiences from Two International Organizations

OWINO NISA OCHIENG

There has been a dramatic change in managerial functions since most international organizations were established to deal with the political, social, and economic issues of the post–World War II era. The trend reflects a more competitive yet demanding environment, the growing complexity of sociopolitical problems, and a change in organizational philosophy, from asset management to operations management. At a time when these organizations are faced with the enormous tasks of dealing with and settling complex global and regional problems of every nature, management must base strategic decisions more than ever on human resources (HR) considerations—matching skills with jobs, keeping key personnel after reorganization, and solving the human problems that arise from introducing new automation and structures, most of which are being demanded by member countries.

For the purposes of this book, it is imperative to provide some general definition of the topic: setting up and operating an internal consultancy facility. An internal consulting unit is one that is established within an organization—national or international—to provide consulting services to other units of the same organization. Deviations and delimitations are not very precise. These services are given many different names, but the term management services prevails. Such units can be found at different places in the organizational structure. Some of them provide consulting services in the full sense of the term; they have a mandate to intervene in an advisory capacity at the request of top management or a unit manager within the organization. In other cases, consulting is one of the staff functions, and the units concerned are also responsible for developing and maintaining accounting and information systems, records and reporting procedures, organizational circulars, staff development programs, and other similar functions.

The growth of internal consulting has been impressive in recent years. Internal units undertake many types of assignments that used to be given to external consultants. Having some sort of internal management consulting service has become common practice in international organizations. However, it is surprising that until around 1980, neither the African Development Bank (AfDB) nor the United Nations (UN) had internal consulting units. In 1980, the AfDB unit was established temporarily, to deal with expected changes. The unit was staffed with technically competent specialists and generalists, some of whom were trained by an external management consulting and accounting firm, Price Waterhouse International. The reaction to the establishment of an internal consulting unit by line managers in the AfDB was one of resistance or fear of change.

The primary purpose of establishing internal management consulting units is to make consulting available to many internal units and departments to deal with problems for which they would not otherwise have had access to consulting expertise. Other reasons for establishing an internal management consulting facility are quick availability; knowledge of the organization's practices, work and management style, culture, and politics (hence sensitivity); a more rapid orientation in any work situation; and confidentiality. Internal management consulting is often thought to be more appropriate for problems that require a deep knowledge of the highly complex internal relations and constraints in an organization.

Independence and objectivity certainly present a problem in some cases. This occurs if the responsibilities of management and the internal consultants overlap, if consultants are used for anything that comes into an executive's mind, and if the consultants know that they have to please top management rather than giving an impartial view. An internal management consulting service that has low status and has no access to top management will not be able to deal with high-level and interfunctional problems, and its recommendations will lack credibility and authority. If, on the other hand, the role and status of the internal consulting unit are properly defined and respected, the independence, objectivity, and credibility of this service can be considerably enhanced.

The use of internal consultants is not a passing fad; nor will it replace the use of external consultants. The latter will continue to be preferred in situations in which an internal consultant does not meet the criteria of impartiality and confidentiality or lacks expertise. However, it is difficult to contest the view that internal consulting has a definite role to play. Its obstinate opponents would do well to stop denigrating its potential.

Experience in the African Development Bank and the United Nations

What follows is a description of the author's firsthand experience with the processes of institutional reforms involving the setting up and utilization of internal consultancy facilities in two international organizations: the African Development Bank and the United Nations. There is an obvious preponderance of material on the AfDB mainly because of the uniquely interesting nature of the developments in question.

In the case of the African Development Bank, assignments were entrusted to joint teams of external and internal consultants. This was a technically interesting arrangement. It reduced costs, helped external consultants to learn quickly about the bank, facilitated implementation, and contributed to the training of internal consultants.

The external consultants enjoyed working this way and regarded internal consultants as useful technical partners. In many situations it was tactically better if proposals were endorsed or presented by an internal unit than if they represented only an outsider's view. Internal consultants were involved in defining terms of reference for external consultants, establishing short lists for selecting consultants, making the selection, negotiating the terms of contracts, discussing recommendations, and monitoring implementation.

It was thought then by the top management of the bank group that the competence and credibility of internal consultants could be increased by involving them in matters pertaining to external consulting. The bank group was particularly interested in establishing, in the long run, performance improvement, technique, and staff training programs that might be of interest to member countries. The bank group envisaged other opportunities for making effective use of the cooperative relationship within the bank. A good example is advisory missions of senior line managers and professional staff to national governments that were members of the bank group.

The kinds of activities in question were not normally referred to as consulting in the real sense of the term. However, the exercise tended to produce better results if the individuals involved were familiar with principles and methods of conducting internal professional consulting.

Changes and Difficulties

The internal consulting service brought numerous changes to the AfDB related to planning and implementing the basic operations of the bank. The organizational change, however, was fraught with difficulties and pitfalls.

The primary function of internal consultancy was to bring about changes, but the behavior of the consulting staff generated resistance to change and initially brought the whole process to a standstill. To defuse this negative behavior, the line managers, consultants, and the whole body of staff were provided with in-house training to raise their awareness of the complex relationships involved in the change process. They were taught how to approach change situations and to help the rest of the staff cope with the intended changes.

It should be understood that the idea of change implied that there was a perceptible difference in a situation, a staff, a work team, an organization, or a relationship between two points in time. The bank group did not want to change for the sake of change, but rather because it was part of a wider process of development, and it had to react to new environmental changes, constraints, requirements, and opportunities. For the bank group, the changes involved:

- The basic setup of the bank group (administration and personnel, financial operations, economic development, legal counsel, sources of finance and investment);

- The management structure and process (internal organization, work flow, information systems, decisionmaking, control procedures);

- Organizational culture (values, traditions, informal relations, influences and processes, management style);

- Personnel (management and staff employed on the basis of their competence, attitudes, motivations, behavior, effectiveness);

- Organizational performance (financial, economic, social) and organizational adaptability; and

- The image of the organization in business circles and among its member countries.

In the African Development Bank, change was expressed at four levels: (1) knowledge changes, (2) attitude changes, (3) individual behavior changes, and (4) group or organizational behavior changes.

The resistance to change was based on the unknown. Personnel resisted and tried to avoid changes that would leave them worse off in terms of job content, conditions of work, work load, income, personal power base, and the like. Most personnel remained unconvinced that the changes were really necessary. This was mainly due to the fact that the purpose of these changes had not been explained to them. The general personnel viewed the prevailing situation as satisfactory and the effort to effect change as useless and upsetting. The staff also viewed these changes as threatening, especially since they were being imposed without a chance for them to democratically express their views.

The internal consultants believed that, in a world where technologically induced social and other changes were taking place rapidly, top managers and consultants could ill afford to overlook the fact that both the staff and the organization were badly in need of not only stability and continuity but also purposeful change. Striking the right balance between change and stability and helping top management maintain this balance throughout the bank group was one of the vital tasks of the internal consultants.

The AfDB staff wanted to know what the proposed changes were so that they could influence the changes that concerned them directly. Top management and line managers were aware of this fundamental demand and reacted to it by adopting a participative approach to change. Top management, the line managers, and the consultants communicated to the staff who would be affected by specific measures that were being prepared. As a first step, the consultants held preliminary consultations about changes that were about to be introduced. Directors of departments and chiefs of divisions were asked to liaise with the staff in identifying the need for change and in checking whether staff members would react negatively to the proposed measures. Suggestions and criticisms were solicited in order to enable management to reconsider its plan for change on the basis of these data.

It was clear from management's standpoint that it was necessary to press on with the proposed changes. Thus, top management sought the active involvement of both line managers and staff in planning and implementing change. They were invited to participate in defining what needed to be changed and how to do it, and in putting the agreed changes into effect.

In the United Nations (Department of Public Information/Office of Human Resources Management), the proposed changes required negotiation with both the staff and the staff union. It was envisaged that the negotiations would lead to a compromise that neither top management nor staff considered an ideal solution. However, the probability of gaining the support of all concerned, and hence the probability of implementing the agreed-on changes, were enhanced. Both management and the consultants in the UN were aware of the desirability of a dialogue with staff members and staff representatives, not only in cases explicitly stipulated by staff rules and regulations or General Assembly mandated resolutions, but whenever changes might affect the interests of staff and when staff union support might be essential.

Structural Arrangements

In the African Development Bank, organizational structural arrangements were the responsibility of management, which had to decide which specific measures to take in effecting organizational change. No special structural arrangements were made for which additional costs and labor were needed.

What was significant with regard to structural arrangements was the emphasis placed on personnel arrangements—the duties and responsibilities attached to each unit. The organization was expanding its volume of operation and had to define the functions of each unit, division, and department. AfDB managers and consultants had access to a wide range of intervention techniques with which they were able to facilitate growth and change in personnel and the organization as a whole.

Training and Development

Although many of the techniques for assisting change were behavioral science–based and emphasized change in attitudes, values, and relationships, the top managers of the bank group and the UN secretariat placed top priority on training and development, which would provide comprehensive programs for improving organizational performance.

It should be noted that, at first, many top managers and line managers in the AfDB did not believe that training and development could assist organizational change and promote a high standard of performance, particularly among professional staff. It was, however, the view of the internal consultants that if training and development were properly designed and used, they could constitute a powerful technique for change in the bank group.

Management workshops and training seminars, both internal and external, were mounted for management and staff, respectively. These were envisaged as a tool to assist managers and staff to appreciate the need for change and to sensitize them about opportunities, environmental constraints, and the various options available to the organization and to individual staff members. The workshop sessions and training seminars helped bridge the gap between management and staff.

Perhaps the most interesting and efficient—though least formalized—method in the case of the AfDB was the development of bank group personnel through direct cooperation with the internal consultant team on problem solving. The AfDB staff was trained in specific techniques such as time measurement, statistical quality control, and standard costing. Because a number of staff members had to be trained, this necessitated a precisely defined and scheduled training program that preceded implementation.

A number of approaches were deemed possible in the AfDB and the UN:

- On-the-job training by the internal consultant team (AfDB).

- Training of trainers (UN).

- Training of selected staff members from each of the departments, divisions, and units who would, in turn, train the remainder of the staff in their respective offices (AfDB).

- Formal training within the organization, with courses being run by external consultants. In some instances, special trainers were brought in; in others, training was run by the organization's internal trainers (AfDB and UN).

- Participation of selected staff in external training courses (AfDB and UN).

The ultimate measure in the case of both institutions was to create a staff development program as a tool to solidify changes. As the complex problems tackled by the AfDB became increasingly understood, the related training and development of staff also became more difficult to design and organize. The training assignments were aimed at the entire professional and technical staff and related to major changes, for example, extensive reorganizations.

At the AfDB, training was supplemented by programs aimed at maximization of the bank group's efficiency in its capacity to mobilize resources and lend large sums of money to its member countries. This situation required change of attitudes and behavior on the part of both management and staff. The programs in question included in-house seminars, working groups, discussion groups, and special project teams.

Another important feature of training in connection with setting up and operating an internal consultancy facility in the AfDB was that it generated interest in further training and self-development. The same could be said of the UN's experience. Sound management and foresightedness in relation to the future development of these two international institutions stimulated and nurtured such interest. This may actually be the most lasting impact on the concept of internal consultancy.

Implementation

The most difficult part of setting up and operating internal consultancy is the implementation of reforms recommended by the internal consultants.

This is the stage where the internal consultants really want to see proposals for changes not only well received by staff but put into effect with good results.

In the AfDB, it was viewed that without an implementation stage, the internal consultancy process could not be regarded as complete. The solution lay in devising a suitable arrangement involving both top management and staff members. The effect of implementation was to create new tasks and abolish old ones.

In the UN, the staff members' commitment and participation could not be solicited without specifying their contribution either directly or through their staff representatives. Such a specification was particularly helpful in drawing up a training program and in establishing controls for monitoring implementation.

Obviously, various technical and resource factors, especially in the AfDB, had a bearing on the pace and lead time of implementation. As a matter of principle, the internal consultant teams were aiming for a smooth implementation of the changes. The implementation program was defined in the AfDB as controllable and, if possible, measurable results of individual tasks, operations, and steps.

In the UN a good deal of new methodology was involved, leading to preparation of a manual for guidance in the procedure to be followed. Virtually all forms of reorganization, irrespective of their functional or interfunctional aspects, required simple instructions on how to operate them. New job titles, duties, and functions had to be redesigned.

Evaluation

As part of the consulting processes in both the AfDB and the UN, it was imperative to have effective evaluation by joint teams of selected representatives from both management and staff. Their purpose was to establish whether the assignments for change had achieved the intended objectives.

The managements, as a matter of fact, had specific interests and viewpoints. In the AfDB, the management evaluated not only the assignment but also the consultants and their performance. How much of this information was shared was a matter of confidence and judgment. In an assignment that is a true collaborative effort, the evaluation should usually be open and constructive.

Information Management

The restructuring of the AfDB as a development organization was concerned with the division of tasks and responsibilities among the entire staff, the assignment of tasks and staff to each unit, the definition of vertical and horizontal information flows and collaborative relations, and arrangements for coordination. The purpose of restructuring was to provide a more or less fixed and stable framework for an effective functioning of the total bank group in achieving organizational goals.

To help with the realization of the bank's restructuring, a management information system was established. It comprised defining information required for strategic management and operational control, harmonizing and integrating systems used in various departments, and choosing and introducing appropriate information-processing technology (and training the staff to manage it). This work concerned both external and internal information. The purpose was to make sure that management did not ignore information that was essential for strategic and operational decisions, while avoiding the collection and development of information that was of no direct use.

In the UN, the structural changes (better known as reform) required tremendous collaboration between staff and management; information that could be obtained to reorganize the UN had to be approved by the General Assembly before it could be put into effect.

Conclusion

It should be understood that setting up and operating internal consultancy in these two international organizations required a lot of work. In the case of the UN, the staff union played a key role in protecting the interests of its members. Whatever changes were made, the staff interests had be taken into consideration without violating contractual agreements. In the AfDB, the situation was different, although some form of internal dialogue was deemed necessary, and considerable training activity had to be conducted in order to guarantee the success of the reforms.

PART IV

Country Experiences

CHAPTER 14

Experience in the Use of Management Consultants in Tanzania

WILLIAM H. SHELLUKINDO
AND SAMUEL K. MTALI

Upon attainment of their political independence, many African countries established economic and social infrastructures that needed able management in order to achieve their development objectives. Only few of these objectives have been realized, however, partly due to a dearth of managerial skills. Tanzania has not been spared from this problem. The problem, in Tanzania's case, was further compounded by the promulgation in February 1967 of the Arusha Declaration, a national policy of socialism and self-reliance whose effect was, among other things, to bring all the major means of production under state control. As a result, the country was forced to staff nationalized, strategic institutions with nationals whose managerial capabilities left much to be desired. Very few of them had university education, and hardly any had the necessary managerial experience. In filling some of the positions that require high levels of specialization, Tanzania sought and obtained assistance from other independent African countries, such as Nigeria and Ghana, under the policy of Africanization. As more Tanzanians were trained and gained the requisite experience, the Africanization policy was phased out to give way to the policy of localization, under which nationals were appointed to managerial positions.

Against this background of a managerial class lacking in long-term professional experience yet manning important national institutions, management consulting has been a very useful tool. It has helped to re-invigorate the performance of practicing managers and civil as well as military administrators.

In the following pages we outline Tanzania's experience in the use of management consulting services in the postindependence period. It is our aim to shed some light on how indigenous talents in management consultancy can be optimally utilized.

The Management Consultant

A management consultant is an expert or specialist in management issues, practices, and techniques who uses that expertise to help clients solve their managerial problems. The consultant acquires such expertise through training, practicing, and long exposure to management problems as a manager, a management trainer, or a consultant, backed by the right formal education. Our experience in Tanzania shows that most of the management consultants are university graduates in commerce, finance and accounting, engineering, economics, law, administration and management, sociology, and psychology.

In developed countries, most management consultants are retired management practitioners. But in Tanzania, and perhaps in many other African countries too, the consulting profession has not been the pre-serve of retired management practitioners or those of advanced age. Young university graduates have also joined the management consulting career. Since age and maturity are associated with experience, we may assume that many chief executives in both public and private enterprises refrain from using indigenous management consultants because of the latter's alleged lack of experience.

Theoretical Role of a Management Consultant

The management consultant, as a specialist in the management field, is expected to help clients solve their practical management problems and thereby achieve desired goals. The terms *help* and *desired goals* are crucial in the consulting activity and in understanding the consultant's role. The consultant is basically a helping hand to the management of an organiza-tion, valuable for his objectivity in analyzing problems, issues, or situations.

Theoretically, the consultant's analysis has to strike a balance between client satisfaction and avoidance of bias. This is in addition to the consultant's goals of earning a fee and maintaining a good reputation.

As a helper, the consultant's success depends on the initiative and cooperation obtained from the client. The client must be clear about what he wants to achieve from the services of the consultant. Consequently, the client must frame the terms of reference to the consultant quite clearly in relation to the problems, issues, or situations for which the consultant's services are being sought. The client must promptly furnish the consultant with the right information and be readily available for discussion throughout the exercise. In the quest for solutions to the problems of the organization, management and the consultant must work closely together.

Historically, however, the role of a management consultant has been that of an expert who, upon being called in by a client, carries out a study, prepares and submits a report, and leaves. The consultant in this case has indulged in a "selling" mission instead of helping the client with his problems. This style of consultancy is common among the so-called briefcase consultants, or consultants with no fixed abode. In fact, when recommendations based on studies made without the participation of the client have been implemented, the results have been so adverse that the whole package of recommendations has been shelved and the assistance of another consultant sought. There are a few briefcase consultants in Tanzania. In the majority of cases, these are people who have failed elsewhere or have been retired from their jobs due to violations of codes of conduct and have sought refuge in management consultancy. This chapter does not address this category of ill-famed management consultants.

Practice of Management Consulting in Tanzania

Need

The operation or performance of any institution—be it a government ministry, a parastatal organization, or a private enterprise—is influenced by the environment within which it operates. The environment, which can be political, economic, legal, social, or a combination of any of these, is dynamic in character and can influence operations positively or negatively, depending on the nature of the activities or functions undertaken. Successful chief executives constantly adjust their operational systems in order to cope with the ever-changing environment and, to do so, they normally consult experts to ensure that their organizations run as effectively and efficiently as possible.

Experience shows that most managers are eager to see their institutions achieve their objectives. Nevertheless, by the nature of the managerial function, most of these managers encounter such numerous problems that they hardly have time to appraise their performances and plan their operations with a view to coping with the ever-changing environment. Where they have time, they are constrained by a lack of competent personnel. Even when competent personnel are available, management's ability to tackle an organization's problems will be constrained by an insider's bias. The hiring of external management consultants thus becomes inevitable. By their nature, management consultants objectively analyze the problems of their clients, assess their causes, work out solutions, and eventually assess the implementation of the recommendations made.

At times, management executives would like to introduce changes in their organizations to enhance performance. Owing to lack of appropriate expertise and experience, however, they may find it difficult to make the right decisions about what changes would be most appropriate. Where the desired changes have been identified, the executives may still fail to come up with the best way of introducing them. In such situations, management consultants have been very helpful.

Currently, there is a strain on management consulting services in Tanzania due to expansion of management activities that call for the adoption of high-level management techniques. Inefficient and ineffective management of public enterprises has caused great concern in the government, leading it to impose consultancies on organizations that are not performing well. Rescue operations consisting of commissions, task forces, teams, and panels of management specialists have been used to analyze problematic management situations with a view to rectifying them. Those in charge of such organizations have invariably viewed such a course of action as unwarranted interference with their managerial functions. Government, on the other hand, has justified its actions in terms of its accountability to parliament and, through the latter, to the tax-paying public, which may be called upon to bail out mismanaged public enterprises.

We suggest that the safest way out of such official interference is for the managements of these enterprises to adopt management consultancy as an ongoing operational technique. It is gratifying to note that, in fact, a few public enterprises have already signed agreements with indigenous consultants or consultancy firms that have helped keep their operational systems under constant review.

Policy Guidelines

It has always been the policy of the government of Tanzania to encourage both public and private institutions to seek professional advice in order to improve their performance. The government has also encouraged the establishment of professional service organizations for the purpose of providing expert advice to institutions that need it. Of all the professional service organizations, the management consulting profession has been established late in comparison to such professional services as law and engineering. Thus, Tanzania has many legal, architectural, and engineering consulting firms. Some of the older ones have even managed to form professional associations.

Despite government encouragement, it was not until the mid-1970s that management consulting firms, both public and private, started to mushroom in Tanzania. As far as the establishment of public management consulting firms is concerned, tribute must be paid to the International Labor Organization (ILO), the United Nations Industrial Development Organization (UNIDO), and the United Nations Development Program (UNDP) for their assistance in establishing the famous National Institute for Productivity (NIP) and the Tanzania Industrial Studies and Consulting Organization (TISCO). NIP and TISCO are both public institutions.

Before the mid-1970s, foreign management consulting firms had obtained government clearance to operate in the country and tap the Tanzanian market. Foreign private firms, mostly based in Western Europe, were the first to capture the Tanzanian market. Coopers and Lybrand Associates Limited, incorporated in the United Kingdom, was one of the first consulting firms to open permanent offices in Tanzania. Later, North American firms, such as Arthur D. Little and Mackinsey and Company, won assignments in the country. These North American firms operated from their bases in North America. The Tanzanian market is still open to foreign management consulting firms. Consequently, new foreign consulting firms, such as MacRastor A.B. from Finland and Norplan A/S from Norway, have established strong bases in the country. Nearly all these firms have employed high-caliber local consultants.

In order to control the influx of foreign consultants, the government has directed that any foreign management consulting firm wishing to operate in Tanzania, or any local institution wishing to employ a foreign management consulting firm, must get approval from the Public Management Development Council (PMDC). Before granting such approval, the PMDC consults local consulting firms to ascertain that the required expertise is not available within the country. On several occasions the PMDC has turned down requests for the employment of foreign consulting firms on the grounds that the expertise sought was available locally.

It was actually around 1974 that public institutions started to seriously get into management consulting. That was the time when NIP was restructured to undertake management consulting activities. During the same period, the then Industrial Development Centre (INDCENTRE) was transformed into TISCO.

As the role of management consultants gained acclaim, the government, through the Management Training Study (MTS) conducted in 1975, issued policy guidelines regarding the undertaking of consulting services in the country. The guidelines explicitly authorized all management training institutions in the country to undertake management consultancy. The MTS recommended to the government that:

- Public management should be encouraged to attempt to solve its own operational problems before resorting to consultancy.

- Large organizations should be encouraged to build up their own consultancy capacity.

- The government should look to the university and the other management training institutions as the primary resources for consultancy.

- Each senior management training institution should be encouraged to develop its own area of specialization and its own special clientele for consultancy services.

- National issues requiring major multidisciplinary consultancy services should be organized by the PMDC, drawing the specialized resources needed from the different training institutions.

- In order to ensure that local consultancy capacity is fully developed, all requests for consultants from outside the country should in the future be approved in advance by the PMDC.

After deliberating on these recommendations, the government accepted them and directed management training institutions to be active in management research, consultancy, and authorship in order to make their teaching meaningful, up-to-date, and down-to-earth. Government's support for management consultancy thus sparked management consulting activities at the University of Dar es Salaam, the Institute of Development Management (IDM), the Institute of Finance Management (IFM), the National Institute of Transport (NIT), the College of Business Education (CBE), and the Cooperative College in Moshi. What started off as small management consultancy units are now maturing into full-fledged departments.

Specialization and Clientele

In Tanzania, a considerable number of management consulting firms, both public and private, have been established. These firms specialize in a variety of management activities ranging from accountancy to multidisciplinary management consultancies. The Appendix to this chapter profiles the major management consulting firms permanently based in the country.

Each of the firms shown in the Appendix has, through mutual contacts, established a sizable clientele. Most of the public enterprises and government ministries have turned, for their consultancy needs, to public consulting institutions such as NIP, TISCO, IDM Mzumbe, the University of Dar es Salaam, and, of late, the Eastern and Southern African Management Institute (ESAMI) in Arusha. Private enterprises have sought consulting services mostly from fellow private consultants. For instance, Industrial Management Services (IMS), a member of the famous K. J. Group of Companies, offers consulting services to firms affiliated with the group. The Industrial Promotion Services (IPS) also offers consulting services to the IPS Group of Companies. Likewise, the Board of Internal Trade, which is a public enterprise, offers consultancy services to its associated companies. In any case, quality, specialization, cost, and time factors all influence the decisions of would-be users of consultancy services. It is therefore not uncommon for public enterprises to use consultancy services of private firms, which, though usually expensive, are of high quality and are speedily delivered. However, there are a few good public consultancy firms that offer consulting services to privately owned companies too. These issues are discussed further in the following section.

Experiences in Management Consulting Practice

For some institutions, the use of management consultants has had favorable results; for others, the purchase of such services has caused disappointments. In a few instances, the disappointments have been so disastrous that certain quarters have associated management consultancy with subversion and international intrigue. Following are a few cases drawn from both foreign and local consultancies.

In the late 1960s, when the government of Tanzania was faced with the problem of how best to serve rural areas, it sought the services of an internationally reputed foreign management consultancy firm to devise a viable system for managing rural development. At the end of their field study, the consultants went back to their overseas base to process the data, assemble their report, and draw up recommendations. They came up with recommendations to decentralize the government decisionmaking machinery and at the same time abolish city, municipal, town, and district authorities. The government accepted the report, fully adopted the recommendations, and made decisions for their implementation. In the course of implementation, some people lost their jobs as a result of the abolition of the local authorities. Functions such as agriculture, education, and health care were decentralized. Under the new system, no ministry was allowed direct contact with its regional or district personnel on administrative matters; it had to go through the regional or district development directors. The ministries were allowed direct contact with their field staff only on purely professional or technical matters.

Over time, it became apparent that the decision to decentralize government functions could not achieve all the desired goals and objectives. Moreover, dismantling the structures of rural and urban governments turned out to have been a serious mistake. It became necessary to revisit the earlier decisions and, in the late 1970s, government decided to reintroduce city, municipal, and town authorities. In the early 1980s, the district councils were reestablished, and the post of district development director was eliminated. The lesson to be learned is that since the original consultants were not locally based, they could not assist in evaluating the implementation of their recommendations. Therefore, the entire consultancy package that had cost millions of shillings had to be thrown overboard.

Also in the late 1960s, the government commissioned another firm of internationally reputed management consultants to advise on the improvement of the tourist industry in Tanzania. The reports produced by the consultants were so unrealistically voluminous that the busy managers could hardly find the time to study them in order to make viable decisions concerning the implementation of the recommendations.

The same firm was also hired in the early 1970s to advise on the improvement of the cashew nut industry. The outcome of that exercise resulted in the creation of a number of cashew nut processing factories with funds loaned from international finance institutions. The sad story about this exercise is that the factories operated for hardly five years before closing down due to a decline in cashew nut production. It is quite apparent that the increase in processing capacity was not matched by an increase in cashew nut production. Although the country is struggling to repay the loans obtained for building the processing plants, the consultants are enjoying the fruits of this consultancy and are probably happily consulting for other African countries.

In 1985, when one public enterprise found itself inundated with demands for improved services in the rural and urban areas, it sought the assistance of international consultants. The consultants undertook a management study of the existing organizational structure in view of the increasing demand for its services and the need to establish a subsidiary company specializing in serving the rural areas. The consultant's final report was presented to the client in mid-1986. At the time of this writing, the recommendations contained in the report have not yet been implemented. It appears that the consultants failed to consider a number of factors pertaining to the client's operating environment. It is believed that the client is now in the process of appointing a local consulting firm to go through the international consultants' report and then prepare some operational manuals that would facilitate the implementation of the recommendations.

Of the indigenous public consulting firms in the country, the National Institute for Productivity (NIP) is the oldest. It was established in 1965, followed by the Tanzania Industrial Studies and Consulting Organization (TISCO), established in 1976. NIP started to embark on management consultancy in the early 1970s, and records indicate that it has played an important role in enhancing the efficiency of many public enterprises in the country. The institute has been consulted by the government on various matters, including the reorganization of ministries.

TISCO has been consulted by both public and private enterprises in its field of specialization—industrial management. However, TISCO has recently included some aspects of general management consultancy on its consultancy agenda. The firm has even been able to export its consultancy services to other African countries such as Botswana.

A review of the performance of our local management consulting firms suggests that they have been working hard all along to offer satisfactory services. Despite their commendable performance, however, local consulting firms still need to be given the opportunity to build up their capacities and capabilities and to accumulate more experience. We base this statement on our review of three cases.

The first case is one in which a client requested the services of an indigenous consulting firm toward the end of 1984. Normally, such an assignment should have taken about two months to execute. It actually took the client and the consultants ten months to agree on the terms and five months for the consultants to produce their preliminary report. As of 1987, when this case first came to our attention, the two parties had yet to meet to discuss the preliminary recommendations in order to allow the final recommendations to be prepared. As a result, the consultants have not yet been paid. We gathered through our research that the client was so dissatisfied with the consultants' output that the client decided to maintain diplomatic silence and close the chapter. The client claims that the consultants failed to complete the exercise in the agreed time and that the preliminary report was unsatisfactory in both form and content. It is claimed that the consultants merely reproduced what they had been told by the client. The client's view was that the consultants were not serious and that the consultancy firm's expertise in the subject matter was questionable.

In the second case, a client became so dissatisfied with the local consultant's output that he decided to hire another consulting firm to undertake the whole exercise afresh. In a third and similar case, a local consulting firm was commissioned by a client to design some promotional materials, but two weeks after the commencement of the exercise, the consultant was discontinued in favor of a foreign consulting firm.

These are probably extreme illustrations of disappointment with local consultancy services, but they may be indicative of a problem more widespread than we are willing to admit.

In spite of the foregoing three cases, there are reasons to believe that, on balance, local consultancy firms are better placed to provide good services, provided they are given the necessary encouragement and challenge. After all, Rome was not built in a day.

The foregoing examples refer to services rendered by public management consultancy organizations. It must be noted, however, that individuals within these organizations have also been consulted and given specific assignments, sometimes with highly satisfactory results. For example, in 1979, the Tanzanian cabinet, seeing that many public enterprises and ministries were facing managerial problems, directed the then Ministry of Manpower Development and Administration to launch a vigorous management training program for all top executives in public enterprises, ministries, and regions. Because the ministry did not clearly know the management training needs of the top executives, it sought the help of the University of Dar es Salaam. The university offered the services of one of its reputed specialists in management and administration to study the issue and advise the ministry accordingly. The specialist—a professor—undertook the study and completed it on time. The ministry accepted the recommendations of the consultant and immediately launched the first ever countrywide management training program for top executives.

In order to give the program impetus, the ministry resolved to retain the services of the university professor on a part-time basis. He was made leader of a standing training team established by the ministry to oversee and coordinate implementation of the training program. The actual training was done by ESAMI, IDM Mzumbe, NIP, and the University of Dar es Salaam. The training program is still running on the basis of the recommendations of the indigenous consultant. There are, in fact, many consultancies carried out by indigenous consultants for the public sector, but this stands out as one of the most successful consultancies undertaken by an individual indigenous consultant.

The cases related to foreign management consulting firms, as narrated above, are by no means exhaustive. But these cases suggest to us that local consultants are more relevant; they know the local environment better and are always available to assist in the implementation of their recommendations. What is important is that they are given the necessary support.

Reluctance to Tap Indigenous Consulting Resources

Our research has led us to believe that high-quality consulting services are available within the country. We are, however, aware of the fact that some public as well as private enterprises prefer to use external management consulting firms. These enterprises also tend to use commissions, committees, task forces, teams, and the like to analyze situations and advise on measures to be taken. The government itself continues to use this method. The most recent important commissions appointed by the government include two presidential commissions on the performance of government and the parastatals, popularly known, respectively, as the Hamad and Kisumo Commissions of 1983. These commissions were appointed to review the performance of the public sector in light of the prevailing economic problems. They completed the work and drew up recommendations that were wholly accepted and implemented by the government. Another one, the salaries review commission—popularly known as the Nsekela Commission—was assigned the task of reviewing the salary structure of the public sector. The tasks assigned to the commissions mentioned above could have been undertaken by existing consulting firms and probably in a more methodical manner.

Single parastatals are resorting to the use of task forces to tackle specific management problems. For example, in 1980, one parastatal organization set up a task force to work out an incentive scheme for its workers. Because of inadequate experience, the task force co-opted one indigenous management consultant from a local consulting firm.

Many more examples of the use of task forces, committees, and the like can be quoted. The question we should ask ourselves at this juncture is: Why have these ad hoc arrangements become so fashionable, in spite of an abundance of indigenous consulting expertise? A quick review of many cases reveals that the general reluctance to utilize available local management consulting services is due to the following factors:

- Some consultants fail to complete assignments in the contracted time, and some who manage to complete the tasks on time produce reports of poor quality.

- There is a general misconception that consulting work is the domain of international consulting firms and that no local firm is capable of producing anything worthwhile. In some cases, a consultancy assignment may be denied if the consultant happens to be a familiar face.

- Local enterprises have a tendency to demand very high standards and qualifications from prospective consultants, thus frustrating local applicants. In some cases, the "came from Europe syndrome" has become a deciding factor in the choice of a consultant.

- Some consultancy assignments are determined, or at least influenced, by donor interests. There is a general tendency on the part of donor agencies to favor consultancy firms from their home countries in the award of donor-aided consultancies. Even multilateral organizations are not bias free in this regard. The World Bank and the UNDP, in particular, tend to involve, as a matter of necessity, international consulting firms in projects they finance.

- Many public as well as private enterprises are unaware of the availability of good-quality management consulting services in the country. For example, TISCO is generally known as a firm that deals only with industrial feasibility studies, although it also undertakes general management consultancies. Likewise, NIP is known to some organizations as an institution for management training, yet it has been undertaking management consultancies for many years. The same applies to other institutions such as the University of Dar es Salaam, ESAMI, IDM Mzumbe, the Institute of Finance Management, and other private organizations whose business names do not mention management consultancy.

- Some enterprises that need consulting services are so financially constrained that paying a consultancy fee equivalent to US $50 day is unaffordable.

- The recent mushrooming of management consultancy firms has given rise to stiff competition for limited jobs, and it is not uncommon for "dirty tricks" to be used in order to earn the scarce consultancy contracts. Some managers find this state of affairs repugnant.

Problems with Indigenous Consultants

Our experience with consulting services in Tanzania indicates that most of the public consulting firms face numerous problems such as lack of trained and experienced staff, inadequate working facilities and conditions, inadequate working materials, poor financial bases, problems with the consultant-client relationship, and limited scope.

Lack of Trained and Experienced Staff

Maturity, or, in other words, accumulated professional experience, is an important factor in the consulting profession. Most management consultants of international repute are people with long working experience in the management field. In Tanzania, the public consulting firms are generally staffed with young university graduates, some with just over two years work experience.

Because there is no special training in consulting services, such young graduates have to learn the profession on the job. Only a few of the consultants in public consulting organizations have previous work experience as managers. Needless to say, a consultant is better able to deliver satisfactory services if his educational qualifications are backed up by extensive work experience in a managerial capacity. Therefore, good training and experience are prerequisites for good management consultancy services.

When the requisite skills and experience are grossly lacking, then there is a tendency for such consultants to use short-cut methods in trying to satisfy clients' needs. As a result, managements are made to purchase the so-called "bags of tricks" that eventually turn out to be "bags of rubbish."

Poor Working Conditions

A consultant needs facilities and working conditions that are conducive to serious thinking and concentration. Lack of reliable transport is a major constraint in the Tanzanian consulting industry; it is not unusual to see consultants walking long distances clutching their "bags of tricks." Looking for office or residential accommodations in Dar es Salaam, where most of the consultants operate, can be a nightmare. In fact, when recruiting new staff, many consulting firms make it clear from the beginning that no issues pertaining to residential accommodation will ever be entertained, and that one should be prepared to share a table with a colleague.

Inadequate Working Facilities

Some very good consultants find it hard to produce their reports due to a shortage of good and affordable secretarial services, good quality paper, and binding facilities. This is aggravated by the limited or complete lack of access to computer and word-processing services experienced by many young consulting firms.

Poor Financial Base

A poor financial base would render any consulting firm incapable of completing assignments on time. The firms in question cannot meet their consultants' transport costs and cannot even buy the necessary stationery for publishing the completed work. Clients sometimes pay consulting firms an advance fee, but the financially constrained firms use the advance to pay outstanding debts and, therefore, fail to start new assignments that have been partially paid for. Some organizations, even when they are aware of problems that require intervention by management consultants, cannot find enough money to hire a good consultant. They will sometimes settle for cheap but professionally mediocre consultancy services.

Consultant-Client Relationship

Due to lack of understanding of the ideal relationship between a client and a consultant, clients tend to treat consultants as if they were magicians. Therefore, they expect them to know the problem immediately and give prescriptions that cure the client organizations' "illnesses." Obviously, the consultancy culture has yet to establish itself among many of our public and private enterprises. There is, indeed, need to demystify management consultancy.

In management consultancy, the ideal relationship is one in which the client and consultant are partners in problem solving. When such a relationship has been established, there is generally mutual appreciation of the problems encountered in the course of the consultancy exercise. Thus the consultant facilitates problem solving rather than solves the problem himself. In this relationship, one is dealing with neither "bags of tricks" nor "bags of rubbish." As a matter of fact, we are in full agreement with French and Bell when they say "Successful [consultancy] efforts involve a process of mutual influence, not an imposed program from any direction. The client and the consultant together will be looking for ways to improve the total [systems]. The real issue, then, is openness. If the client and the consultant are open with each other, the total system becomes a matter of joint concern."[1]

Limited Scope

A quick review of the specializations of the indigenous management consulting firms in Tanzania indicates a limited scope of operation. Many offer consultancies basically in finance and accounting. A few undertake industrial feasibility studies, and others opt for quick result-yielding tasks like the preparation of management manuals. Local consulting firms have rarely undertaken large multidisciplinary management consultancy assignments. Such assignments have tended to be the preserve of foreign consulting firms.

It is true that our consulting firms are still in the early stages of learning. Therefore, they need time to acquire the necessary experience. What they now need is the opportunity to grow and expand their scope. All in all, our indigenous consultants need the cooperation of their clients in the battle to stamp out unfounded biases and beliefs, such as the belief that only foreign consultants have the capability to undertake complex management consultancies. At the level of government policy, there should be an endeavor to regulate consultancy activities in such a way that foreign management consultancy firms bidding for contracts within the country are required to use local management consulting expertise. We quote Correa, who wrote:

> For local consultancy firms, the possibility of entering into consortia with extra-regional firms often constitutes a condition for successful bidding. Frequently, tendering conditions include requirement (particularly those related to previous experience) that local firms cannot meet alone; sometimes, moreover, clients, deliberately or not, discriminate against local firms by asking for qualifications or experience that can only be satisfied by international consultancy firms. This behavior is, in some cases, a response to the mistaken belief that imported services are necessarily better than the local ones, or to the lack of an adequate perception of relative advantages that local services may offer vis-à-vis foreign services.[2]

In our opinion, Africa's budding consulting organizations can, if given the opportunity, grow up to provide consulting services that are as good as those offered by any foreign consultants.

Need for Positive Action

The cases cited above lead us to suggest some courses of action that would create conditions for the optimal utilization of our indigenous management consulting capacity. These suggestions spring from the fact that, first, foreign management consulting firms tend to be favored over local firms. Some chief executives mistakenly assume that good experts are always foreign. Second, some executives have not yet tested the advantages of utilizing management consultants. This may be a problem of ignorance. They are surrounded by a multitude of managerial problems but they do not see how a consultant can be of help, particularly when the consultant is a local person. Third, some consulting firms are not well known to their would-be clients. Many consulting firms have not publicized themselves in the public media, ostensibly for reasons of maintaining consulting ethics. In view of the foregoing, we suggest that:

- Regular management workshops be arranged and conducted by selected training institutions or associations to emphasize the advantages of utilizing management consulting firms in tackling management problems, with particular emphasis on the use of the abundant indigenous expertise. The initiative of the African Association for Public Administration and Management (AAPAM) in this regard needs to be emulated.

- Indigenous management consulting firms should be assisted to form national associations of management consultants. These would constitute a forum for the consultants to establish a professional code of conduct or ethics, plan training workshops for practicing consultants, and establish joint strategies for tackling problems affecting the management consulting profession. Such associations may advise governments on whether foreign management consulting expertise is required for specific tasks.

- When foreign consulting firms must be brought in to undertake assignments, it should be obligatory that they work together with indigenous consultants. This would facilitate transfer of consultancy know-how from the foreign firms, and in the process, help create a strong indigenous consultancy base.

- As far as possible, local management consulting organizations should be given the opportunity to handle large and multidisciplinary management consulting assignments. Thus, the relevant policy regulations should be revised to give preference to indigenous consulting firms in awarding assignments.

Appendix

Name of Firm	Field of Specialization
Industrial Management Services (IMS) P.O. Box 21001 Dar es Salaam Tel. 31453	General management Financial management and 　accounting Project management
Industrial Promotion Service Ltd. (IPS) IPS Building P.O. Box 9241 Dar es Salaam Tel. 24334 or 20483	Project management Feasibility studies Finance and accounting
Sting-Back Ltd. Management Consultants P.O. Box 1109 Arusha Tel. 3075	Financial management Accounting Auditing
Massawe and Company Accountants 　and Auditors P.O. Box 2475 Dar es Salaam Tel. 20930	Accounting Auditing
Kaka Advisory Services Management Development 　Consultants P.O. Box 997 Dar es Salaam Tel. 31789 or 21999	Financial management Accounting Auditing Tax planning Production management Marketing studies Materials management Personnel management Corporate secretarial 　services
Trion and Company P.O. Box 997 Dar es Salaam Tel. 21999	Auditing services

Name of Firm	*Field of Specialization*
University of Dar es Salaam Faculty of Commerce and Management P.O. Box 35091 Dar es Salaam Tel. 48168	Financial management Marketing management Production management
Management Investment and Tax Consultancy Ltd. Ohio Street P.O. Box 1043 Dar es Salaam Tel. 30556	Investments management Taxation
Institute of Finance Management (IFM) P.O. Box 3918 Dar es Salaam Tel. 27171	Finance management Accounting Insurance management Taxation Materials management Project management
Institute of Development Management P.O. Box Mzumbe Morogoro Tel. 2401	General management Financial management Marketing management Production management Workforce studies Accounting Project management Management training
Nyegezi Social Training Institute P.O. Box 307 Mwanza	Financial management Accounting Taxation Materials management Marketing management
Norplan A/S P.O. Box 2920 Dar es Salaam Tel. 48221 or 48403	Projects management Economic studies

Name of Firm	Field of Specialization
Cooperative College P.O. Box 474 Moshi Tel. 2228 or 3220	Financial management Accounting Cooperative management Economic studies Marketing research
National Institute of Transport P.O. Box 705 Dar es Salaam Tel. 48328	Transport management
Eastern and Southern African Management Institute (ESAMI) P.O. Box 3030 Arusha Tel. 2881	Transport management General management Training needs identification Financial management Accounting Economic studies Workforce planning Health management Management training
M-Konsult Ltd. P.O. Box 2711 Dar es Salaam Tel. 38713 or 38714	Project appraisal Project management
Sykes Insurance Consultants Ltd. P.O. Box 1615 Dar es Salaam Tel. 20886 or 20448	Insurance management
Board of Internal Trade (NIT) P.O. Box 883 Dar es Salaam Tel. 28301	Accounting Corporate planning Marketing research Workforce studies
M.K. Consultants P.O. Box 5612 Dar es Salaam Tel. 26117 or 30153	Marketing research Project management Business administration

Name of Firm	*Field of Specialization*
Associated Business Consultants P.O. Box 3361 Dar es Salaam Tel. 28336	Insurance management Pension management
Norconsult P.O. Box 9620 Dar es Salaam Tel. 6074	Feasibility studies

General Office Equipment and
  Marketing Consultants
P.O. Box 5568
Dar es Salaam
Tel. 30766
	Marketing
	Maintenance of office
	  equipment

Institute of Sales Promotion P.O. Box 616 Dar es Salaam Tel. 50377	Sales management Sales promotion and advertising
J.V. Projects and Management Ltd. P.O. Box 4162 Dar es Salaam Tel. 31075	Project management Financial management

Notes

1. Wendell L. French and Cecil H. Bell, Jr., *Organization Development: Behavioral Science Interventions for Organization Improvement* (Englewood Cliffs, NJ: Prentice-Hall, 1978), chapter 17.

2. Carlos Maria Correa, *The Use and Promotion of Consultancy Joint Ventures by Public Entities in Latin America*, ICPE Monograph Series No. 18 (Ljubljana, Yugoslavia: International Center for Public Enterprises in Developing Countries, 1985; distributed in the U.S. by Kumarian Press).

CHAPTER 15

The Gambia's Experience in the Use of Management Consultants

S. M. B. FYE AND DONALD C. SOCK

It is now generally accepted that Africa's problems relating to development will not be solved by development assistance alone. Management efficiency in the control and utilization of scarce resources and in the initiation and execution of development policy constitutes a major determinant of progress and prosperity. It is not surprising that management consultancy has not developed into a major profession of great relevance for Africa.

This chapter highlights experience gained in the Gambia in the use of indigenous management consultants. The issues and problems raised are essentially drawn from experience in three major government ministries—the Ministry of Economic Planning and Industrial Development, the Ministry of Local Government and Lands, and the Ministry of Education, Youth, Sports, and Culture—and from the Management Development Institute of the Gambia.

The chapter is divided into three sections. The first section discusses why different government agencies utilize the services of indigenous management consultants. The second discusses the actual experiences of different government agencies and some public- and private-sector organizations and the reasons for success and failure. The third section addresses ways and means of encouraging optimal use of indigenous management consultants.

It is important at the outset to be clear about definitions. In this chapter, the term *indigenous management consultants* is used to refer exclusively to two categories of management consultants: (1) African consultants hired by government, public- or private-sector organizations in the Gambia to deal with specific management problems within a short specific period; and (2) Gambian consultants hired from similar agencies and training institutions to deal with specific management problems. Consequently, the term excludes experts recruited through technical assistance programs to undertake relatively long assignments or studies lasting longer than a year. The term also excludes experts and consultants drawn from the developed countries, particularly Europe and the United States.

The term *management consultancy* similarly needs to be defined to avoid confusion and misinterpretation. Management consultancy is not an established or exact science and, consequently, a universally acceptable definition is impossible. The definition offered by Alfred Hunt states that "management consulting is an organized effort by specially trained and experienced persons to help management solve problems and improve operations, through the application of objective judgement."[1]

The Institute of Management Consultants in the United Kingdom defines management consulting in broadly similar terms: "the service provided by an independent and qualified person or persons in identifying and investigating problems concerned with policy, organization, procedures and methods, recommending appropriate action and helping to implement these recommendations."[2] Both definitions describe the management consultant as an independent, objective specialist with skills and attributes essential for diagnosing a specific management problem and helping to provide solutions. The reality in many African countries, including the Gambia, is that this image is not always correct. From the standpoint of client organizations, management consulting can be defined as "the temporary infusion of outside and credible talent, to provide new ideas to an organization by performing various problem-solving activities, while trying to maintain high professional standards and at the same time trying to serve the special interests of the client and the consultant."[3] This chapter relies on this last definition.

Reasons for Engaging Indigenous Management Consultants

Since the launching of the first National Development Plan in 1975, the use of indigenous consultants to undertake specific assignments has significantly increased, particularly in the areas of structural reorganization of diverse sectors of the public service, project planning and implementation, human resources development and utilization, and institutional reform of public enterprises.

Before 1970, no comprehensive planning was undertaken in the country, and the periodic preparation of a public-sector capital budget (funded mainly by two donor agencies) provided the major thrust for development. Sectoral policy and targets remained uncoordinated, and national planning machinery was nonexistent. The public service was, in the words of its head, "in a state of crisis and inertia, plagued with deficiencies inimical to change and progress."

Experience during the first plan period, 1975–80, fortunately dispelled some of these deficiencies. The level of planning consciousness and discipline rose very sharply and permeated several sectors of the economy. An elaborate national planning machinery provided popular participation in the development effort. At the apex of the system was the National Planning Council, with the President of the Republic as chairman. A Development Review Committee, headed by the Minister of Economic Planning and Industrial Development, closely monitored the progress and impact of national development projects and policies. The close involvement of the nation's leaders in the development process (enhanced by the increased support and assistance of thirteen donor agencies) stimulated marked changes in the attitude and orientation of top-level management in the public service. The prudent management of the nation's meager resources and the transformation of the public service into an efficient instrument of change and progress became major preoccupations of top-level management. The review of procedures, methods, and organizational structures and objectives became a central concern. Since expertise in the field of management was limited, many ministries were obliged to engage the services of indigenous management consultants.

In the Ministry of Economic Planning and Industrial Development, ten indigenous consultants (funded mainly by multilateral agencies—the African Development Bank, the World Bank, and the Economic Commission for Africa) were recruited for short-term management assignments between 1975 and 1980. The problems they addressed included establishment of management information systems for project implementation units, procedures for reporting on progress in implementation, guidelines in project design and appraisal and the conduct of feasibility studies, and diagnosis of training needs for administrators, planners, and professional technical staff in managerial roles and positions.

In the local government sector, the major areas of concern were decentralization and its implications for financial control and accountability and ministry and departmental relationships, reorganization of the community development services, and different aspects of land administration, with particular emphasis on allocation and utilization procedures.

In the Ministry of Education, Youth, and Sports, indigenous management consultants have been utilized since 1975 to advise on the reorganization of the Department of Youth, Sports, and Culture and the formulation of a youth policy, the establishment of an effective inspection unit for educational services, the management of the control and supply of educational materials to schools, and the management of school meal programs.

There are five major factors that prompted the use of indigenous consultants by government agencies and private-sector organizations. Each is discussed below.

Impartial Viewpoint

Even senior executives who are intellectually and professionally equipped to offer sound management advice or analysis of specific problems often lack the time to devote to such an exercise. Besides, they may be too influenced by their personal involvement in existing traditions and habits to see problems in their true perspective and offer objective solutions. The basis for this contention, as Dr. M. Kuls puts it, is that "it is difficult to concentrate on operational and conceptional problems simultaneously."[4]

Politicians and decisionmakers tend to entertain prejudices against local experts and officials, simply because they are too involved in day-to-day operational problems and concerns. Unfortunately, the views of local experts often have to be expressed by distant "objective" and "dispassionate" consultants to win credibility or acceptance.

Justification of Predetermined Measures

Public officers and politicians are frequently confronted with situations that require them to resort to unpopular decisions. The removal of subsidies on rice and fertilizer, introduced in the Gambia in 1986, was a major political decision, fraught with sociopolitical risks. A donor-funded consultant had to be utilized (after the government was already committed to the policy) to analyze the problems of subsidzing of agricultural commodities and reduce public opposition to the policy. Similarly, in 1979, the introduction of a cattle tax to encourage the sale of cattle to the Gambia Livestock Marketing Board had to be preceded by a consultant's report to increase motivation for the sale of cattle and to discourage the use of cattle as mere symbols of status and wealth.

Avoidance of the Issues

Indigenous consultants have been utilized to temporarily divert attention from issues that the government was not adequately prepared to address or resolve. Between 1975 and 1980, at least three consultants and three committees were set up in the Gambia to investigate the problems in land administration and to propose remedial measures. A perusal of the reports that resulted from these exercises confirms the similarity of diagnosis and prescriptions. Before the consultants were recruited, the Gambian public was generally incensed by (1) the allocation of one plot of land to five to ten different people, (2) allocation of plots to fictitious names and minors, and (3) violation of areas of land reserved for the creation of greenbelts and other public amenities, including markets, schools, parks and play fields, highways, and cemeteries. The consultancy exercises were seen by members of the public as bold and positive steps designed to resolve problems of national concern. The reports that emerged from the studies provided government with sufficient justification to make the inevitable decisions: (1) dismissal of the Minister of Lands, (2) suspension and later dismissal of heads of departments and some officials involved in land administration, and (3) withdrawal of plots that were not provided with leases.

In this particular exercise, the consultancy assignments proved unnecessary and superfluous. The investigations hardly disclosed anything that was not already known, and the recommendations that were finally implemented had been consistently advocated by senior officials who were familiar with the land problems.

Familiarity with Socioeconomic and Cultural Milieu

Since independence in 1965, there has been a marked tendency to give preference to indigenous management consultants. Experience in the use of non-African consultants has not been very satisfactory. Many of them came with predetermined notions, prescriptions, and prejudices, which provoked resentment and hostility from local officials. More seriously, many lacked familiarity with the socioeconomic and cultural milieu, a factor that adversely affected the accuracy and relevance of their analysis and prescriptions. African consultants are generally seen as allies, coming from similar backgrounds and situations, who are consequently better equipped to understand our problems and concerns. Unfortunately, experience has shown that some African consultants are equally distant and alienated, analyzing our problems from the perspective of Western values and beliefs.

Special Knowledge and Skills

The indigenous consultants utilized over the years generally possessed the required skills and expertise to investigate the management problems identified by different government agencies. Most of them had undertaken other consultancy assignments in different areas of management and in countries with similar circumstances and problems.

In recent years, attempts have been made to utilize local management trainers as consultants for government ministries and agencies. The Management Development Institute has undertaken two government consultancy assignments for the Ministry of Agriculture and the Ministry of Local Government and Lands. These assignments were encouraged by both government and donor agencies for the purposes of reducing the dependence on external consultants, enhancing the Institute's capability in the area of management consulting, and facilitating the implementation of consultants' recommendations. In both assignments the Management Development Institute offered to assist the agencies in implementing the recommendations and to undertake any additional exercises that might be required. External consultants are not generally available to assist in the implementation of their findings and recommendations.

Experience with Indigenous
Management Consultants

The Gambian experience with indigenous consultants has been varied.

The Good

Many of the major development projects that have significantly contributed to increased social welfare, better distribution of income, and increased agricultural productivity have been designed and implemented with the assistance of indigenous consultants. The Irrigation Rice Development Project in the MacCarthy Island Division, which has significantly increased the income and food security of over 3,000 Gambian farm families, owes much of its success to the efforts and expertise of indigenous African consultants recruited by the African Development Bank—one of the principal funding agencies for the project. The management structures and institutional arrangements that facilitate the active participation of female farmers in particular, the flow and sharing of valuable information, and the management of the implementation process were installed by African management consultants working in an environment and culture similar to those in their home countries.

Similarly, the design and implementation of the institutional arrangements for the National Primary Health Care (one of the successful projects in the Gambia) have been guided and facilitated by the management skills of indigenous consultants recruited by the World Health Organization (WHO). These experts demonstrated tremendous capacity to work within the sociocultural framework, to build on the strengths offered, and to minimize the negative effects or disadvantages. The African consultants who worked on this project insisted on the widespread use of social and cultural organs to disseminate information and to mobilize popular support and participation. Similarly, traditional channels of authority within villages and districts were strengthened and followed. This policy helped bring project officials, supervisors, and project beneficiaries much closer together.

The reorganization of ministries in the public service has benefited from investigations and reports undertaken by various Economic Commission for Africa (ECA) consultants including Dr. J. Balogun, Mr. E. F. Efange, and Dr. Wamalwa. The efforts of these consultants were not confined to the production of reports alone. Several of them maintained close ties with the senior officials of the government and took pains to monitor progress in implementation. Several also returned to the country to participate in workshops and seminars that offered opportunities for the elaboration and justification of management advice tendered in reports.

Indigenous consultants have demonstrated their capacity to work under difficult conditions and with insufficient resources. The organization and management of the 1983 census in the Gambia were undertaken by African consultants willing to spend long periods in remote rural areas to test questionnaires, establish organizational procedures, and initiate sample studies and surveys.

The achievements of indigenous consultants regarding the management of public- and private-sector organizations have been equally impressive. The National Investment Board, which has responsibility for coordinating and supervising public investment in the country, has utilized indigenous consultants to set up such enterprises as the National Trading Corporation, the Livestock Marketing Board, the Gambia Tannery Company, and Citrus Products Limited. Indigenous consultants provided the management skills and expertise that led to the creation of improved management structures and systems in some of these organizations and in the major parastatal agencies, such as the Gambia Produce Marketing Board, the Gambia Port Authority, and the Gambia Cooperative Union. Indigenous consultants have, in several cases, involved local officials by seeking their views and advice, particularly on matters pertaining to organizational cultures, leadership styles, and national ethos. In this manner, indigenous consultants have helped develop the skills and experience of local counterparts in the area of management consultancy. The close involvement of local officials in consultancy assignments also facilitates the implementation of consultancy reports.

In the field of institution building, the record of indigenous consultants has been impressive. The creation of the Management Development Institute in 1984 and the design and development of its core programs have been facilitated by perceptive studies and analyses offered by short-term consultants. The reports of indigenous consultants helped develop the existing partnership between the managers of the public service and the management of the institute, which is essential for the relevance of programs and the effectiveness of training.

The Bad

Although indigenous consultants have played positive roles in our national development efforts, they have also created serious problems for the public service in particular. Contrary to the popular belief that they are generally objective and independent, there have been instances in which their reports were influenced by a desire to extend assignments or undertake subsequent studies, to create unnecessary jobs for friends, and to avoid sensitive or controversial issues.

In 1986, two indigenous consultants were recruited by WHO—one to examine how to make the administration of the Royal Victoria Hospital in Banjul more efficient and the other to investigate the integration of the Ministry and Department of Health and Medical Services. The former recommended, among other things, the creation of a Management Board for the Banjul hospital to provide overall policy direction and guidance, and the delegation of many mundane day-to-day duties to the hospital administrator. One of the resulting benefits was to free doctors and specialists for more professional activities in the hospital. The expert recommended a follow-up study on the administration of the other major hospital in the country, located about 320 kilometers from Banjul. After careful consideration, the government decided to create a similar management board for Bansang Hospital after the necessary legislation was passed by parliament. The follow-up study recommended by the consultant was found to be totally unnecessary and was consequently rejected.

The second consultant, after presenting the case for integration, recommended a management structure that was very expensive to operate and relied heavily on the advice and support of externally recruited management consultants. It was consequently discovered that several of the recommended candidates had often worked with the consultant in assignments abroad. The government considered the elaborate and expensive management structure unnecessary and rejected the creation of many of the posts recommended by the consultant.

Consultants have sometimes been found guilty of departing from the terms of reference assigned to them and producing reports that have been either irrelevant or grossly inadequate. In 1980, the Ministry of Local Government and Lands had to abandon a report that was supposed to examine the feasibility of amalgamating the Surveys Department, the Land Office, and the Physical Planning Department, because the focus was on land administration problems. The central issue of creating a viable organizational structure by amalgamating the three departments was hardly addressed or analyzed. In this particular exercise, the terms of reference prepared for the consultant turned out to be imprecise and too open-ended. The consultant was required to examine over twenty issues raised in the form of a questionnaire. The determination of the issues that were of major concern to the organization were virtually left to the discretion of the consultant. He was also required to categorize the twenty issues raised in the questionnaire into a few broad areas of concern.

The formulation of terms of reference in this manner creates all sorts of confusion and makes it difficult for the consultant to distinguish the forest from the trees. Conversely, when terms of reference are scrupulously prepared by top management to address specific and major areas of concern, consultants tend to find themselves in straitjackets. They lack the flexibility to investigate other related areas that might offer insights that are vital for the diagnosis and treatment of the organization's disease.

The question of whether terms of reference should be short, specific, and explicit or broad and comprehensive to permit further explorations by the consultant has been a baffling one for Gambian top management. Many managers find it difficult to pinpoint the problems that create poor performance in the organization: inefficiency, inadequate motivation of staff, and so on. The problems that manifest themselves may reflect the symptoms of the illness but not the real disease. Since the quality and adequacy of terms of reference virtually determine the quality and relevance of consultancy assignments, top management is now devoting more attention to this area. Several managers now resort to diagnostic surveys, during which a consultant is brought into an organization to identify the real problem facing top management and then draft the terms of reference for a consultancy assignment.

The inadequate supervision or monitoring of consultancy assignments has compounded the terms of reference problem. Very often, government agencies initiating consultancies do not take sufficient interest in the effective monitoring and delivery of the service. Many consultants are not supervised or monitored and are not periodically called in for consultations, review, and feedback. Top management is often either too busy or engrossed in other activities (including foreign travel). The result is that by the time reports are submitted, ministries have very little ownership of the consultant's findings and recommendations.

Another problem has been the tendency of some indigenous consultants to unduly consume the meager resources of government organizations. Many have been known to exploit ministries and departments to provide logistical and material support not covered by their contracts. The demands made for free secretarial and other services, when added together, can be substantial and create resentment and antagonism. Extravagance in the use of government resources sometimes leads to unrealistic estimations of what government can afford. Many consultancy reports have been shelved by various government agencies simply because the government could not afford to implement them. The financial implications of the implementation of recommendations are not always addressed, and when they are addressed, the usual cliche is: "Government is required to mobilize the required funds to put these recommendations into effect."

The steps that must be taken by government or the Ministry of Finance to mobilize the resources are seldom pursued. A major weakness of indigenous consultants has been the tendency to overestimate the level of management consciousness in the public service and in the country in general. Management development and training in the Gambia are still in their infancy, and most organizations still operate on the basis of routine and traditions. The concepts of management efficiency, management by objectives, and administrative reforms have not yet gained widespread acceptance and support. There is still a tendency on the part of top management to view consultants with suspicion and skepticism. Many managers refuse to cooperate with consultants because they believe that the consultants are out to discredit their organizations and policies, to create trouble, and to sanction their replacement or removal. In this prevalent atmosphere of suspicion and skepticism, consultants have to be extremely tactful and should manifest a good deal of interpersonal and interactive skills. Unfortunately, some of the indigenous consultants recruited in the past have not possessed these attributes and did not fully understand or appreciate the level of management consciousness. This led to frustration and mutual hostility, which eroded the value and benefits of some consultancy assignments. In some public- and private-sector organizations, consultants are believed to look for opportunities to increase taxation, to reduce fringe benefits, and to stop loopholes that lead to illegal enrichment or corruption. Consequently, every effort is made by top management in such cases to frustrate consultancy assignments.

Optimal Use of Indigenous Consultants

Since optimal use of indigenous consultants is broadly addressed by other authors in this book, only brief comments are made here. First, the evidence in the foregoing pages confirms that African governments need to develop a sound and articulated policy on the development of management consultancy. Many countries do not have a clear and well-defined policy in this area. Second, there is a need to develop training opportunities for local management consultants. Officials with the potential and aptitude for special courses or training programs in management consulting must be identified. Third, top management responsible for the recruitment of consultants has to be trained how to monitor consultancy assignments and prepare terms of reference. This is the only way to dispel the popular belief that "consultants come in to tell you what you already know, put it all into a long report that no one reads or reacts to, and have the effrontery to borrow your pen to write out the bill."[5]

Notes

1. Alfred Hunt, *The Management Consultant* (Toronto: John Wiley & Sons), p. 6.

2. *Guide to Membership* (London: Institute of Management Consultants, 1984).

3. Larry E. Greiner and Robert O. Metzger, *Consulting to Management* (Englewood Cliffs, NJ: Prentice Hall, 1983), p. 9.

4. M. Kuls, in M. Kubr, ed., *Management Consulting—A Guide to the Profession* (Geneva: International Labor Organization, 1978), p. 9.

5. Hugh O'Neil, *The Training of Consultants*, p. 7

Index

AAPAM. *See* African Association for Public Administration and Management

Acceptance, *See also* Credibility; Indigenous consultants; of indigenous consultants, 41–42

Accountability: consultancy review for, 170; in IHL consulting, 100; of indigenous consultants, 60

Accountant, external. *See* External accountant

Accounting firms: African, 50–51; in Kenya, 50–52; and management consulting, 13, 49; multinational, 48–49

Accounting services, indigenous consultants for, 40

Accounting system, for consulting firm managers, 89–90

ADB. *See* African Development Bank

Administrative Staff College of Nigeria (ASCON), *See also* Institutions of higher learning; Nigeria; consultancy work of, 153–54; consulting experience at, 17; objectives of, 152; training programs of, 111, 154

Advertising. *See* Publicity

African Association for Public Administration and Management (AAPAM), 2–3, 24, 33, 39; on attributes of good consultants, 10

African businesses. *See* Management; Private sector

African consulting. *See* Indigenous consultants

African Development Bank (ADB): and African consultants, 1, 40; and Gambian agricultural development, 192; internal consultancy

History, *See also* Foreign consultants; Multinational firms; of African consulting, 46–51; of Eastern and Southern African Management Institute, 138–39

Host countries, *See also* Donor; Foreign consultants; problems with foreign consultants, 59

Hostility, in consultancy environment, 35, 196

Human resources management: and organizational effectiveness, 8; strategies for utilizing, 156

Hunt, A., consultancy definition of, 188

Hyden, G., 7

Ideology. *See* Politics

IHL. *See* Institutions of higher learning

Illiteracy, of working women, 71

ILO. *See* International Labor Organization

Immigrant communities, *See also* Foreign businesses; technical monopolization by, 47

Implementation and control, for consulting firm managers, 89

Incentives, for private consultancy, 5–6

Incorporation, for university consultancy unit, 99

Independence. *See* Postindependence

Indigenous consultants, 1–2, 6, 10–13, 25–26, 37–42, 55–56, *See also* Client; Management; Professionalism; advantages of, 14, 28, 35, 53–55, 60–61, 106, 176, 188; attributes for, 10, 32–34, 75; and client relationship, 33–36, 109–11; complaints of, 41–42, 176; definition and role of, 38, 87, 168–69, 188; in desegregation

cases, 48; experience opportunities for, 42–43, 53–54; and foreign consultants, 1, 2, 11, 40, 43–44, 51–52, 64, 92, 146; in Gambia, 187–96, 190–92; government promotion of, 81–82; and IHLs, 96–97; and internal consultants, 156–58; in Kenya, 50–53; in Nigeria, 16; organizational forms for, 82–86; origins and traditions of, 46–50; and private sector, 5–6, 14–15; and private sector consultancy, 5–6, 14–15; problems with, 2–3, 11, 40–42, 61–63, 179–81; and problems with managers, 29–31, 61, 146; professional procedures for, 88–92; remuneration and payment criteria for, 87–91; requisites for, 10, 30–33, 44–45, 53, 87; specialization of, 38–39, 192; in Tanzania, 172, 179–81; utilization of, 28, 38, 58, 149, 177–79, 196–97

Indigenous managers. *See* Management

Industrial Development Centre (INDCENTRE). *See* Tanzania

Industrial Management Services (IMS), and K. J. Group, 173

Industrialization, *See also* Development; and foreign consultants, 28; gains in, 24; and institutional changes, 81

Inflation. *See* Economic recession

Informal sector, *See also* Formal sector; Private sector; women workers in, 73–74

Information, *See also* Communication; Feedback; in client-consultant relationship, 115–16; "live channels" for, 15; for report process, 119–20

Information gap, for indigenous consultants, 12